THE FIRST TIME DAD SURVIVAL GUIDE

SIMPLE TIPS FOR EXPECTANT FATHERS TO CONFIDENTLY SUPPORT THEIR PARTNER DURING PREGNANCY AND PARENTHOOD TO BECOME THE WORLD'S BEST DAD

HARMONY BROOKS

TABLE OF CONTENTS

INTRODUCTION

Before I got married I had six theories about raising children; now, I have six children and no theories. –

JOHN WILMOT

Welcoming a little baby into your life is a transformational adventure of a lifetime. As they say, when your baby is born, you are also reborn. Becoming a father for the first time is sure to evoke a million different emotional responses. While the excitement of having a child is always palpable around expectant and new parents, so is the anxiety. From stirring moments of watching your baby's little toes wiggle to exhausting moments of changing the diaper in the middle of the night, a baby will change everything.

The preparation starts from the day you know your partner is pregnant. You are not alone if you ask these questions: "My wife is going through so many changes; how can I best support her?" "Can I help her through the throes of pain as she delivers our bundle of joy?" "The baby is here; what am I supposed to feed them?" "How do I soothe them when they cry?" From choosing a name for your baby to selecting the best doctor(s) and gynecologist(s), the sense of responsibility dawns like the plot of some Christopher Nolan movie on you. The day you know you will be responsible for caring for this little angel, you may focus more on your financials, future planning, and saving. Everything you ever knew about the world and yourself will be challenged. You will be pushed every day to become the best version of yourself and the best dad! Your life and time will revolve around your baby, and it's understandable to want to learn as much as possible before the baby arrives.

While some of it can look like the most beautifully crafted dream, some of it comes with its own set of worries. For example, the continuous testing and increased frequency of medical visits, though crucial for monitoring the health of your baby and partner, can also become a stressful experience. For the duration of waiting for the results, you and your partner can go through difficult emotions and anxious anticipation.

Nervous? That is understandable. Remember when you first went to school, had your first job, or took that big step to get married? You did it all, and you can do this too. All it will take from you is patience, understanding, and curiosity to learn about your baby's developmental stages and how your partner's body is transforming.

Pregnancy is not just about your partner undergoing hormonal and physical changes but also an opportunity to take your relationship to the next level. In these nine months and beyond, you will no longer be simply life partners but co-parents. This brings another set of challenges as well as life-altering experiences.

Differences in parenting approaches are natural, as humans seldom agree on everything. For example, what kind of diet is best for your baby seems like an innocuous question at first, but when both parents read diverse literature, they can sometimes disagree on what and whom to follow! Things become even more confusing when you get exposed to contradictory information. Even medical professionals can offer differing advice. However, to give a nurturing environment to your baby, navigating those differences and cultivating the skill to achieve consensus becomes paramount.

I can assure you that if you are feeling anxious about the gravity of this responsibility, you are not alone at all. Caring for a baby is a full-time responsibility; sometimes, you and your partner can feel overwhelmed to the point of burnout. Of course, you will want to be present for everything all the time, and talking about self-care can come across as a tad bit selfish. However, it is equally important to be mindful that your physical, emotional, and mental health counts.

Ultimately, happy homes raise happy children. To that end, I want to share with you that being exhausted all the time need not be inevitable. Sharing the responsibility of being a parent and allowing yourself the time to rejuvenate go hand-in-hand.

Sounds good, but how can you do this? Sure, there are no rigid rules on how to achieve balance, but this is exactly where your mutual love and the desire to raise a happy kid can help. Seeing unity in your goals can prompt you to explore a common path that works for both of you.

In an information-rich online environment, you can find many resources for all your questions and concerns. But, at the same time, the amount of information and diverse sources containing useful knowledge can be overwhelming. And, you're right, there is so much to do! Where to start?

Don't worry! You can start here. In this book, you will find the answers you are looking for in a systematic and easy-to-understand manner, all in one place. Additionally, you will explore and learn certain tips and tricks to help you navigate the journey of fatherhood and be a rock-solid support system to your partner. This book will serve as an informative resource and be your companion for the rest of your beautiful journey. Think of it as your portable little best friend!

The following chapters begin from the moment you receive the good news and take you through the nine months and the birth experience that comes after. From navigating the newborn phase to sharing your roles and responsibilities, here you will find valuable information on striking a balance between family and work life, dealing with parental concerns, and managing your time for self-care, all while being the best dad!

Are you ready to be the best dad? Let's do it!

CHAPTER 1
THE JOURNEY OF FATHERHOOD BEGINS

Congratulations! That pregnancy test was positive and you are going to witness a profound and magical tale unfold in the next few months! Just how magical are we talking about? Let me tell you...

It had been a grueling 14 hours, after which Cathy and Jacob had their baby boy arrive in this world and draw his first breath. As Jacob took his baby in his arms, he couldn't help but let go of all the emotions that had been bubbling up inside him. As his baby cried, as babies do, he cried too. In that moment of pure joy, Cathy wondered who the baby looked like out of the two! She also wondered what was going on between the father and son as they gazed at each other.

Sometime later, Cathy would ask him what holding their baby for the first time felt like. Jacob answered, "A tiny red blob with sparkling eyes that I would love and protect fiercely for the rest of my life; so much love."

For Jacob, the fear of seeing his partner in so much pain and, at the same time, wishing for his baby to be delivered healthy was combined with the astonishment of seeing the miracle of birth. A million thoughts rushing through his mind were silenced the moment he held his baby for the first time. All that washed over him was love; so much love for this little life that had existed for just over a few minutes, and yet, feeling like he had always been a part of their life.

That is the kind of magic we are talking about—the creation of life in its most raw form and realizing that you are responsible for it.

Suppose you connect with first-time dads anywhere in the world and ask them what they felt when they first held their child in their arms. In that case, their answers will surely be different, but they will all have one thing in common: an intense and instant sense of an emotional connection characterized by love, gratitude, and anxiety. For example, Danielle Campoamor (2016) writes about new dads feeling a range of emotions when they hold their babies for the first time. From feeling thankful for healthy deliveries to being speechless and emotionally overwhelmed, they all experienced unbound joy.

But, hang on a minute! Love and gratitude, we understand, but anxiety? It is quite natural to feel anxious, especially if you are a first-time dad, due to all of the expectations and stereotypes surrounding the whole experience. It's also equally natural to feel afraid of the future because, at that moment, your tiny baby is completely dependent on you for its survival. The weight of that responsibility is enormous. Not only are you now responsible for your child, but you also need to keep yourself in the best health and mental state to take care of your child to the best of your abilities. Furthermore, there is anxiety over the fact that the world is not a very kind place, and as your child grows, they will have to navigate this world.

These myriad thoughts running in different directions can come to you not only when you hold your baby for the first time, but even before that! That's right. The journey of fatherhood begins at the moment of conception, long before you are aware of it. What can you do? Read on to find out how you can support your partner through this journey by navigating expectations and stereotypes and setting up a solid foundation for being the best dad.

EMBRACING EXPECTATIONS

Chances are, you're tired of hearing, "Hey! Your life is about to change forever." Of course, you know that. But, how exactly will your life change, and in what ways? Knowing this beforehand can bring you a lot of clarity and prepare you for when the baby arrives. Getting acquainted with some of the expectations from a new father can help you figure out your own path to an awesome fatherhood.

Less Spontaneity, More Planning

Even before the baby arrives, you will likely be expected to take a lot more things into account before making any spontaneous plans. Co-living with a partner already involves shared plans, but with a baby on the way, the dynamics change a lot more. For example, you two enjoyed spontaneous date plans, but now your schedule will revolve around how your wife is feeling, both emotionally and physically, with all the changes that will happen to her (hormonal and more).

What else? You would not want to miss out on the routine medical check-ups and the important know-how from those appointments just because you feel like hanging with the guys! No, of course not. With the growing responsibility to support your partner through the nine months and beyond, you both will act like a unit. Additionally, you will be an important pillar for your family that must be present in potential emergencies.

Along with this, financial planning will become second nature to you. From supporting your family to considering medical costs before and after delivery and buying baby stuff, spending will become a conscious and mindful activity for you. You will also start thinking about the distant future of your child, such as funds for their education. While that time is quite far at the moment, you will naturally find yourself thinking about this.

Don't worry; this is not to scare you or your partner but just to highlight that a baby truly makes you a family unit. Knowing that you want to be constructively and lovingly involved in the whole process will make embracing this change easier than you think.

Possible Sleepless Nights

Your baby will have the time of their life by not sleeping while you do! One of the first things to become mindful of is that your time will not solely be yours anymore, and you will have to learn to prioritize your time and tasks, especially to balance work and family.

Babies, especially newborns, spend most of their 24 hours sleeping, but the catch is that their siesta sessions are divided into one or two hours at a stretch. This means that while they will sleep a lot, they will do so throughout the day, which means you will do so too. At about three months, your baby *may* start to sleep for five hours at once (Downs, 2014). If you're having twins or more, you can count on your sleep schedule to be thrown out the window! This only presents an opportunity to enter a collaborative time-management arrangement with your partner.

While it can become difficult if you have a time-intensive job, sharing the responsibility by taking turns and talking openly about how best you and your partner can support each other's sleep needs can work wonders. So, get together, possibly plan for how you expect to handle your sleep schedule, have that conversation, and take the first step of being an awesome dad: sacrificing a bit of your sleep for your baby!

Time Management and Prioritizing Tasks Around Home

Time management for you will go beyond collaborating on sleep schedules. It will permeate all aspects of your life. One of your most important expectations will be to prioritize your tasks around the home and your family, whether it's accompanying your wife to the doctor's appointment or taking care of the baby while your wife sleeps.

Babies grow daily, and small things can change, making you not want to miss anything. As an involved father, you will want to notice every little thing your baby does and be awestruck by the cute antics, expressions, and adorable baby talk.

Being aware of this expectation can come in handy as you make mental notes (if they work for you) on managing your time between home, work, and your baby. Not everything will be equally important to you and call for your attention. The baby will become the priority. This means whatever you were habitually spending your time doing will transform.

Eating, Burping, Pooping, Anytime

Did you know that your baby's stomach is the size of a marble when they are first born? You read that correctly, and it continues to grow daily (Christiano, 2023).

This means that their eating, burping, and pooping schedules are very different from us adults. Because the baby is tiny with tiny organs, their nutrition input and output frequency is obviously more than ours.

Your baby will eat more and their diet will change every three months based on their growth phase. Breastfeeding newborns initially feed somewhere between seven to nine times a day, then around six times as they grow from three to six months and begin their solid food intake (Christiano, 2023). The same goes for their pooping schedule. Another reason to get into that time-management habit and learn diaper-changing skills!

Your Friend Circle Will Change

As Taylor Calmus comically expresses in his 2022 book *A Dude's Guide to Baby Size*, your friends who don't have children of their own yet may not be able to relate to your changed responsibilities, and those who do will understand it all as they will be in the same boat as you.

The point is that, with a new baby, new and qualitatively different kinds of friendships will be on the horizon and some of your old friends may not be as frequently involved in your life as before. This is not something to fear but accept as a natural part of life, as it's part of stepping into a new phase of your life.

Understanding the Quintessential Protectiveness of Parenting

If you've been one of those cool dudes who has an easy-going attitude toward life, prepare to surprise yourself! Remember all the times you have been annoyed at your parents worrying over you incessantly? Or, all the times when they were overprotective to the level of being overbearing? Yeah, you may start relating to them a little more.

While this sounds like the cliché "you will understand once you are a parent" kind of situation, something shifts within you when you become a dad. While we will discuss the science of oxytocin in a while, it is safe to say that as your dad instincts take over, you will understand and relate a lot more to the weight of responsibility and love that makes you want to offer the world to your child and protect them fiercely.

Surprises Regardless of the Preparations

While all these wonderful things can make your heart go all warm and fuzzy, it's important to stay realistic. When the baby arrives, something will get out of hand no matter how prepared and organized you are. It is important for you to remember at that moment that there is no fixed know-it-all manual of parenting.

You may feel guilty for being exhausted with all the childcare, or you may be caught completely off-guard by something that you haven't researched yet. The point is that anything can happen, and you can start feeling overwhelmed as a result. Remind yourself that you and your partner are both human. Feeling intense love for your baby and wanting to be there while being completely exhausted is natural. It is natural for both parents to want to have time just for themselves, together or individually. There will be days that are difficult, but they will pass.

While it feels reassuring to have it all figured out, the truth is that, with parenting, a lot will require quick and on-your-toes thinking. That's alright. That's part of the rollercoaster. Embrace the expectation that all of your expectations can be broken, but with love and understanding, it will all be worth it!

UNDERSTANDING YOUR PARTNER: ESTABLISHING SUPPORT

The pillar upon which a successful parenting partnership is based has to do with a genuine openness to learning about and understanding each other's experiences as a parent and your expectations from each other as well as the whole process. Here are a few things you can try that will help deepen your relationship with your partner. Think of them as an informal guide or pointers to give you a general feel of how to proceed. Remember that there is no final absolute manual on this and relationships are a work in progress. We all grow through trial and error, learning and evolving.

Firstly, the key here is understanding your partner's perspective and needs. Every pregnancy is different and, while some basics stay the same for all expectant mothers, everyone has unique experiences and concerns that make their pregnancy their own. What else? This uniqueness is not limited to your partner alone. As a dad-to-be, this journey will also have a unique imprint for you. So, come on over, huddle up, and listen: *Acknowledging and validating this uniqueness is the best way to show your involvement and support.* So, *Communicate and listen openly with empathy* to your partner.

Secondly, there is nothing more reassuring than providing emotional support through affirmations, compliments, and encouragement. Chances are, your partner already feels conscious about the way they are feeling and looking physically (more so in later months of the pregnancy), and all those stereotypes about body image can really stress her out. In such times, it's important to remember and talk about how the human body is incredible in adapting during pregnancy, which is nothing less than a biological miracle. Affirming her experience and encouraging her can boost her mood and confidence. You can also compliment her on her resilience for putting her body through so much to bring a new life into the world.

Thirdly, expressing your love verbally and through actions can really bring you two closer and make your partner feel supported. Often in co-living situations, also known as marriage, more time together runs the risk of becoming a "taking each other for granted" type of situation. One cannot overemphasize the importance of taking the time to make each other special. Go the extra mile, say the unsaid, and express love verbally and through actions.

Fourthly, *the way forward is active engagement and taking initiative around the house with chores and responsibilities.* Take the example of Maria and Seth. Seth was so enthusiastic about pregnancy that he often asked their doctor many questions to understand how Maria's body would change through the months and what that would mean for the baby. However, he also asked Maria a lot of things about how her body felt throughout the day and tried to understand her discomfort, cravings, and mood swings. His inquisitiveness was genuine, and Maria was more than happy to make sense of her emotions by expressing them to her husband. Once Seth got an idea of the general pattern of his wife's needs, he would be prompt in thinking in advance and fulfilling them. Their fridge always had mint chocolate chip ice cream, and their house smelled of lavender essential oil (Maria found the fragrance especially soothing). You get the idea, right?

Lastly, be *present*. From doctor's appointments to preparing for the baby's arrival, the more you are present on the scene, the more connected you will feel to your baby and partner. Accompany her to doctor's visits, go to parenting workshops, prenatal classes, or that Lamaze class (a class for preparing for pregnancy and birth)! Do things that teach you about both pregnancy and childbirth. Learning something together can be a powerful experience of emotional support. However, being present goes further than this. It encompasses total emotional, mental, and physical support. On the days your partner is physically exhausted or feels discomfort, you can offer her massages or draw her a warm bath. Such simple steps reflect your thoughtfulness and will go a long way in truly establishing a collaborative pregnancy experience.

SETTING UP THE FOUNDATION

Now that you have a basic roadmap for setting up a supportive and fun pregnancy experience, we can focus on more foundational questions. What comes next is a huge step forward, and dividing all your concerns into smaller categories and goals can help make things manageable. This part revolves around a few basic concerns. Let's look at them one by one.

Prepping the Home and Other Practicalities

There will be practical aspects of preparing for the baby's arrival. These include planning and prepping the home for the baby and investing in baby supplies like a crib, diapers, formula, medicated creams, clothes, swaddle blankets, and so on. There are many resources available online that can help you create handy checklists for different tasks and essential items. We will discuss these in more detail in the next chapter.

Collaborative Parenting

This is perhaps the most important part because it directly impacts the kind of environment you will create for your baby. Upbringing styles affect the growth and development of your child and play a role in how they relate to themselves, their parents, and peers (Neilsen, 2023).

Establishing a strong co-parenting relationship and a foundation for shared decision-making is key to achieving a balanced and functional upbringing environment. So, take the time to sit with your partner and discuss all those big things. Explore your parenting expectations and styles. It's essential to remain open and non-judgmental during this time.

This step brings out the different unique strengths that you both possess as parents. In addition, shared parenting is also about shared childcare responsibilities. Listening to your partner, understanding her needs, and expressing your thoughts to her will create a symbiotic sharing of responsibilities. Most importantly, it can help you provide support in the way that your partner needs to be supported.

Shared decision-making also means clearly discussing birthing options and having a birth plan in place as discussed before. You can discuss these things with your medical provider and research different support systems available for pregnant women, like hiring a doula, if that works for your partner.

Establishing a Support Network

Having a support system and network of people to share concerns and seek advice on common everyday questions offers a unique space of reassurance. Other first-time expectant parents, family, and friends can offer you valuable support. People who have been there can share their insights and help you navigate early parenthood phases.

A support system means you will have someone to help you along the path, and you won't have to travel the distance alone. This sense of safety goes a long way in easing stress and anxiety around pregnancy and childbirth.

Education and Research

What do you do when you do something for the first time? That's right, you learn, educate yourself, research, and gain knowledge. Parenthood is no different. Make this your mantra for the next nine months (and beyond): educate, educate, and educate.

There is no such thing as being over-prepared for childbirth. The more you educate yourself, the more informed decisions you'll make even under stressful situations. Yes, it is possible to come across an overwhelmingly massive amount of information that may sometimes contradict something you read previously, but that is all the more reason to go into the research mode and get your hands on various resources.

Whether you're a visual learner and prefer online videos or a reading person and prefer books, be sure to make this a part of your daily routine. Also, who says learning can't be fun? You can create fun pop quizzes for each other with different fun rewards; for example, the winner will choose the next movie you watch together!

Health, Lifestyle, and Work-Life Balance

Good nutrition and a healthy lifestyle are the foundation for a healthy pregnancy and proper development of the baby. Since your partner will be consuming enough food for herself and the baby, her caloric needs will change. As per Johns Hopkins Medicine (n.d.), maintaining a healthy pregnancy requires an extra 300 calories per day, which should be derived from a balanced diet that combines different sources of vitamins, minerals, proteins, carbohydrates, and other nutrients. Folic acid is especially important in the early stages of pregnancy for the baby's development (but more on this in the next chapter).

In addition to nutrition, moderate exercise in pregnancy is encouraged and brings with it many benefits, like better sleep, improved energy levels, improved blood circulation, and reduced stress (Stickler, 2020).

Here are a few things that you and your partner can make a part of your everyday routine (Lewsley, 2021):

- Practice mindfulness activities such as focusing on and awareness of sights and sounds around you
- Meditation and relaxation techniques
- Engaging in conversations and journaling are also helpful, as they can help verbalize and externalize fears and anxieties. Overwhelming emotions, when externalized, can become manageable.

As a dad-to-be, you will also start thinking about striking a work-life balance even before your baby arrives so that you can plan and act accordingly.

Celebrating Milestones, Creating Memories

The journey of being a parent can be romanticized in a million ways. Most of it won't feel like that at the moment as you go by, living your life one day at a time, but in retrospect, all those mundane days will combine to become a story: your story and your family's. Before you know it, you will already be using sentences like, "Honey, remember when..." and it will be priceless!

Make sure you spend quality time with your partner throughout the nine months to celebrate little and big milestones, like the first ultrasound, when you hear the baby's heartbeat, or the first time your partner feels the baby kick. Finding occasions to celebrate together will make your bond stronger and alleviate the stress we talked about before.

You and your partner can come up with your own ideas, but here are some to get you started (Domenica, 2016):

- Celebrate weekly progressions with a nice dinner or a date.
- Create a monthly anniversary celebration of the date you both became aware of the pregnancy.
- Make a picture collection of your baby's ultrasound photographs.
- Document the baby's arrival preparation, for example, pictures of the cute onesies you bought or the nursery you prepared.
- Get creative with your partner's baby bump! You can paint it or make a cast to keep for remembrance purposes.

Now that you know what to expect and how to prepare for your baby, let's get down to the details. It all starts with learning about what physical, emotional, and hormonal changes occur as part of pregnancy to prepare your partner's body for nourishing your child. The next chapter is dedicated to this in detail, and will help you chart out a plan of action for yourself as a supportive dad-to-be.

CHAPTER 2

PREGNANCY 101: NAVIGATING THE NINE MONTHS

You will be surprised to know that up to 80% of men also show physical symptoms of pregnancy! Yes, you read that right. Different studies have pointed out that expectant fathers can experience a sympathetic pregnancy, wherein symptoms like cravings, mood swings, nausea, and weight gain, among other symptoms, can be felt (Rudick & Brott, 2021).

Have you wondered what happens inside a pregnant body? How does the baby undergo different developmental stages?

Let's look at the science of pregnancy and understand how each developmental stage impacts your pregnant partner and baby.

THE SCIENCE OF PREGNANCY: CONCEPTION, TRIMESTERS, AND YOUR BABY

The female body prepares for pregnancy every month through what is known as the menstrual cycle. Think of it as the stages in which the uterus prepares for receiving a fertilized egg and carries the pregnancy in case of a successful conception or shedding the uterine lining if no pregnancy occurs (menstruation or period). A cascade of hormones is responsible for the entire process.

Two hormones are key here: the follicle-stimulating hormone (FSH) and luteinizing hormone (LH). These hormones stimulate the follicles within the ovaries, and every month, one of them releases an egg. This is the process known as ovulation. As follicles mature, another hormone called estrogen is released, which prepares the uterus, as explained above.

Once the egg is released, it has about 24-36 hours to be fertilized by the sperm. Once that happens, the process moves fairly quickly, and the fertilized egg forms a zygote. Rapid cell division occurs at this stage, and the egg travels down the fallopian tube to reach the uterus. The zygote forms a blastocyst and eventually an embryo, implanting into the uterine wall. This embryo will eventually grow and become your baby.

Since there is no precise way of knowing exactly when ovulation occurs and conception happens, the pregnancy baseline is taken from the first day of your partner's last period. A pregnancy generally lasts for 40 weeks and is divided into trimesters to keep track of important developmental milestones (Donaldson-Evans, 2023a).

Let's understand what takes place for your partner and your baby during these nine months and how you can forge a supportive bond with the baby and the mom.

First Trimester

Even when we understand that every pregnancy is different, the first trimester brings with it some common symptoms such as nausea, tender breasts, frequent urination, heartburn, cravings, food aversions, and extreme fatigue. Your partner will most likely feel those symptoms even if the severity is different.

First Month

Generally, the first month of pregnancy is marked by morning sickness, characterized by nausea and heartburn for your partner. The name "morning sickness" is a little misleading as the symptoms can happen anytime during the day or all day. It is unknown exactly what causes morning sickness, but multiple factors, including hormonal changes and increased sensitivity to different aromas, are thought to be responsible.

Your partner will also feel different food cravings, mood swings, sudden outbursts of crying, dizziness, and exhaustion. Given the hormone surge, all these physical and emotional disturbances are natural.

The placenta and amniotic sac will begin to form now. The amniotic sac is a thin membrane-like structure that envelops the fetus as it develops. It is filled with amniotic fluid to protect the baby from injury or changes in temperature. Think of it as your baby's personal cozy snuggle space. The placenta also develops, which provides nourishment and oxygen to the fetus via the umbilical cord. By now, your little baby is beginning to take shape. At weeks 4-5, the spinal cord, brain, and the heart begin to develop. Small buds appear from where the arms and legs will grow.

Second Month

The morning sickness continues this month for your partner. Along with that, tenderness of breasts, tingling in fingers, and increased frequency of urination may occur. Your partner will also feel exhausted at this time. Emotionally, she will continue to have mood swings.

As far as your baby's development is concerned, by the eighth week, your baby's major organs and outer structure will begin forming. Its heartbeat will become regular and rhythmic. By this time, eyelids will also form, arms and feet will grow longer, and toes will appear. Your baby will be one inch long by the end of eight weeks (OASH, 2021).

Third Month

This is the month when your partner's body will start changing ever so slightly. The mood swings will persist, but the tiredness and fatigue will slowly improve. She may feel connected to your baby and continue to form a bond. As her body changes, excitement and frustration can build up. It is important for you to stay supportive of and for her. After all, she is nurturing a life in her womb and expending all her energy doing so!

Your baby's nerves and muscles activate by now, and he can make a fist. His head develops, and he looks more and more like a tiny person. He can also wiggle his toes, make head movements, and open his mouth. Your baby is almost three inches long and weighs an ounce (Rudick & Brott, 2021; OASH, 2021).

Second Trimester

The second trimester is slightly easier on your partner and brings a new wave of well-being. Nausea and physical exhaustion are reduced. However, other symptoms can come up in the second trimester, such as (Mayo Clinic, 2022c):

- Changes in the belly size due to a growing uterus, as well as increased breast size
- Skin changes due to the presence of melanin, darkening of nipples, and stretch marks (fade away after delivery or turn white)
- Braxton-Hicks contractions are irregular and mild tightening in the abdomen that is different from actual labor. However, immediate doctor consultation should be done if the contractions increase in strength and frequency, as that could be a sign of preterm labor.
- Nasal congestion and dental problems
- Leg cramps at night (can be soothed with calf massages, shifting to comfortable shoes, warm bath before sleeping). Or restless legs.

Fourth Month

The symptoms described above will begin in the fourth month. But every experience is different in terms of timing and intensity of symptoms. Therefore, if you openly listen to your partner and understand the patterns of symptoms particular to her, you can support her better through the month.

Your baby has grown up to 4-5 inches now and is the size of an avocado. The development of the heart is completed at this point and beats 120-160 beats per minute. Your baby will be in a position to start swallowing, sucking his thumbs, and kicking. Increased light sensitivity can also be noted by this time. At this point, vocal cords and intestines will also form. Skin will start developing with meconium in the intestinal tracts. Meconium is the baby's first bowel movement after birth.

Fifth Month

In the fifth month, your partner's navel may start to change and pop out as her belly grows to accommodate the baby. There can be occasional dizziness and fatigue, accompanied by swelling of the ankles, fingers, and face. The good news for your partner is that her hair has never been better because of all the surging hormones and improved circulation because of the baby's needs.

Your baby is now six inches in size with fat storage developing under the skin that will give him that quintessential baby-fat cute look! As the growth continues, fingerprints develop, myelin forms (for nerve protection), and reproductive organs start taking their respective place. Your baby will now be covered in vernix, a waxy coating to protect the baby's skin during delivery and after. Lungs and bronchioles are also developing this month. By the end of the month, an ultrasound can reveal the sex of the baby (Donaldson-Evans, 2023c). Around 20 weeks, your partner will have an anatomy scan or target ultrasound, an in-depth ultrasound to check for complications and ensure your baby is healthy.

Your baby has fully grown eyebrows and lashes now, and you can spot some hair on his head. A particularly beautiful possibility of bonding presents here as the baby can now hear sounds outside the womb. You and your partner can try connecting with the baby by talking to him or singing, as babies can respond to such sounds.

Sixth Month

You're getting closer than ever before to the big day now, and your partner will show every bit of it. There will be a greater weight gain with the baby growing increasingly into his final form. This is the time when the pregnancy will make your partner glow but also bring increased sweating, numbness, or tingling in the body. Constant backaches will become more commonplace and are natural, given your partner is carrying an ever-growing baby in her belly. There is also a chance of slight incontinence while laughing, sneezing, or coughing. She may also struggle with carpal tunnel syndrome because of the extra fluid in her body, compressing her nerves (Rudick & Brott, 2021).

Your baby now has a pattern of sleeping and wakefulness and has developed reflexes. As the reproductive organs have formed in the previous months, their development now becomes complete. In the case of a boy, his testicles will move from the abdomen to the scrotum. If you're having a beautiful baby daughter, her uterus and ovaries will shift in their proper place with a complete lifetime supply of eggs.

Your baby's taste buds develop now, and he can swallow small amounts of the amniotic fluid. His eyes start to open, and he can cough or hiccup. He has grown to the size of 12 inches with stronger arms and legs, well-defined facial features, and hair on his head. The bone marrow begins the production of blood cells, and the lungs are fully formed but not functional yet (Donaldson-Evans, 2023d; OASH, 2021).

In terms of recognition skills, your baby now has the ability to form love and attachments to you and your partner's voice. His emotions start to develop. Just like the previous month, the baby is stronger with responses to external stimuli.

Third Trimester

The third trimester is the final leg of the journey: the home run! Now that your baby is gearing up to enter the outside world, he will start taking his final form. The comparative relief of the second trimester will give way to growing discomfort in this trimester as your partner's body pushes its limit to accommodate the growing baby.

Shortness of breath and heartburn are quite common in the third trimester and may be accompanied by swelling in the ankles, fingers, and face. During this time, your partner may feel the baby shifting toward her lower abdomen, and her cervix will slowly become thinner to help with delivery. Her breasts may start producing colostrum, a watery, milky substance. In general, movement and daily tasks may become harder, and your partner may have trouble sleeping due to the discomfort.

Seventh Month

Your partner's hip joints will begin to expand to make room for the growing baby. She will also go through a rollercoaster of emotions as she bonds with the baby and imagines the future, feeling ecstatic at the thought of your little bundle of joy as well as fearful of the labor and delivery process.

As far as your baby is concerned, he is growing ever so strong, reaching anywhere between 15-17 inches in length. Your baby's skeletal structure is fully formed, but the bones are still soft. Lung development is maturing at a good pace, and some practice breathing movement is beginning to happen. Your baby has also started storing some vital minerals, such as iron and calcium. Your baby's brain is developing rapidly, though still smooth. He can also sense the changes in light, and his irises can react accordingly by this month (Rudick & Brott, 2021).

Eighth Month

Since the growing baby is now putting pressure on the organs around the uterus, the shortness of breath continues. Additionally, the pressure on the bladder can lead to frequent bathroom trips, which can be quite annoying. Mentally and emotionally, your partner may reflect upon questions of motherhood (you might also reflect on fatherhood), being a responsive parent, the possibility of how her body may permanently transform or if it can go back to how it used to be, and what will happen to her work life.

In the eighth month, your baby will turn upside-down, with his head pointing toward the ground. This is called the birth position, as babies usually come out head first. However, this may not always be the case, as some babies can come feet-first (breech). Monitoring the baby's position is crucial in later months, especially since breech births can cause problems in standard vaginal delivery and may require a C-section (Cleveland Clinic, 2021).

In the eighth month of pregnancy, your baby is big enough that his movements can become restricted as there is hardly any room left for him to swim around! This means that his movements will be felt less intensely compared to previous months but will still be discernible. By now, your baby is 16-19 inches long and weighs about 6 pounds. Your baby now has an excellent chance of survival after birth.

Ninth Month

Welcome to the last month. This is it! Everything you and your partner have been gearing toward will come to fruition soon.

Not much will differ when it comes to the last month. Your baby's development is complete now, and he is ready to be born any moment as he shifts toward your partner's pelvis. Your baby can now fully practice blinking, head movements, hand movements like clenching and grasping, sucking, and breathing (Crider, 2021).

As your baby's head grows bigger, your partner will continue to feel pelvic pressure. Backaches will be at an all-time high since back muscles work extra hard to support your partner's growing belly. Sleep troubles and exhaustion will continue well until the baby arrives. Interrupted bowel movements and frequent trips to the bathroom will also stay as the internal organs are quite squished by now.

Hold on, dear friend; it will be worth it all as your baby graces your life! Let's look at what role you can play here as an involved and supportive dad-to-be and figure out how to navigate these nine months.

NAVIGATING THE TRIMESTERS

Since the first trimester throws up difficult physical and emotional symptoms for your partner, this phase is particularly troublesome to navigate. However, with much love and care, you can stand by your partner and support her.

Working Through the First Trimester

Nausea is a particularly uncomfortable feeling. Since the sense of smell starts to become profound, you should try to be more mindful and notice your partner's reaction to certain smells. Cravings for certain foods and aversion to others are very common experiences. You can stock up on the kind of ingredients for food that your partner shows an inclination for. It will ease the pressure of guessing what to eat, though cravings and aversions are unpredictable and will continue.

You can load up on healthy snacks so that anytime your partner feels hungry, there is something to quench the hunger (she will feel hungry more frequently because all her energy and nutrients will naturally be utilized for your growing baby). You can also do meal preps and quick meals as part of active engagement in household chores. This will especially provide reassurance for your partner.

As the visits to the doctor will make it amply clear, the importance of a well-balanced and nutritious diet cannot be stressed more. When the doctor prescribes prenatal vitamins, encourage your partner to take them. Your active involvement will mean you ask your medical provider as many questions as required to make informed decisions.

You will also take care of nutritional concerns at this point. Knowing what role each nutrient plays in your baby's development is important. Calcium is crucial in bone development; Vitamin D and magnesium are helpful in the absorption of calcium and guard against preterm labor. Folic acid guards against neural tube defects (in the brain and spine) and is very important in the first 28 days of pregnancy. Similarly, iron, carbohydrates, and proteins are crucial to your baby's development. You can take steps to be proactively involved in healthy and balanced dietary practices.

Navigating the Second Trimester

By the second trimester, there is a greater acceptance of the pregnancy as the reality of it dawns on both you and your partner with more certainty. It is bound to bring many anxieties and fears to the surface emotionally.

Navigating the second trimester is all about getting in the groove of things and keeping the energy and motivation high. There is also much to celebrate and prepare for as time passes, and here are a few things you and your partner can do to shift your focus on the exciting and responsible parts!

Letting People Know

This is the perfect time to start thinking about and planning the birth announcements. Planning how you want to announce your baby's arrival to the world can be a fun activity to do together and can bring you closer to your partner.

Firstly, there can be different mediums you can choose from, for example, online or offline. If you're a bit of a vintage person, you may want to go the traditional route of offline announcements. Be as involved as possible in this with your wife, and think stationary, envelopes, styles, and aesthetics! The good thing is that there are countless ideas waiting for you on sites like Pinterest, which can provide inspiration and ideas, as well as templates that you can use.

Think about what you'd like to include in that announcement. You can get creative here. Of course, you will include your baby's picture(s), but how about a little picture of their tiny hands and feet? Or a cute little piece of paper with their footprints? The creative dimension is all yours!

Thirdly, a celebratory function can be just as much fun! Yeah, if you thought of a baby shower, you're right. Times have changed, and your interest in this book means you have moved beyond the silly ideas of pregnancy-related fun to be exclusive for women! More and more dads are coming on board with the idea of hosting a function such as the baby shower. The joy of receiving cute gifts for the baby and catching up with friends and family while they wish you the best is just beautiful.

Childbirth Education

While fun is great, this trimester is also a good time to get serious about childbirth education. Any education in childbirth, from different approaches to managing pain to stages of labor, will be consequential to you and your partner.

Many people feel uncomfortable at the thought of seeing their partner in pain, especially if there is so much bleeding going on. Understanding childbirth can mitigate that discomfort and allow you to see birth in a new light.

What you will most likely need to do in the beginning is to think about the proper selection of childbirth classes. This will require you and your partner to spend some time researching and talking freely about the philosophy of childbirth you feel comfortable with. For example, many people believe that the natural process of birthing should be allowed to happen without too many interventions. Female bodies are born with the wisdom to give birth, and unnecessary interventions can only create alienation for the mom and baby by taking away the power from the mother (fathers also). On the other hand, some people would like to have epidurals or other pain-relieving medication to ease their delivery. The point is that you and your partner need to sit and have a talk about how you want your baby to arrive in the world.

A birthing class is, therefore, crucial in educating you and your partner on the different techniques and philosophies of childbirth. Some popular approaches to childbirth include the Lamaze method, Bradley method, water birth, and the Birth-Works philosophy, among others (Rudick & Brott, 2021).

The Lamaze method is one of the most popular birth approaches today, developed by Dr. Fernand Lamaze in 1951, incorporating the processes he observed in Russia. The method essentially focuses on relaxation and breathing techniques, along with emotional support by a doula or a close person focused on making the delivery experience as smooth as possible. The philosophy believes women have an innate ability to give birth, and the body's natural urges should be followed without unnecessary medical interventions (Lamaze International, n.d.).

The Bradley method approaches childbirth with the belief that a vast number of pregnancies do not need medically assisted births. With a few things, like a comfortable and familiar environment, dim lighting, emotional support, and confidence in being capable of birthing, a mother can go through delivery without the need for drugs or interventions (Gurevich, 2021).

Similarly, water birth is basically a method where your entire labor and delivery or a part of it will happen in a pool of warm water. It can occur in a hospital or the comfort of your home. Like all techniques, a water birth can be followed after proper consultation with your doctor, which is recommended for a safe delivery experience.

Creating a Birth Plan

A birth plan is like a vision of how you'd like your baby to arrive in the world. It does not mean a watertight rigid plan, but rather a series of ideal case scenarios and their alternatives to be followed in the event of an emergency.

Birth is overwhelming, and medical intervention can become alienating at times. However, having a plan can help manage anxieties by having contingencies in place. It attempts to strike a delicate balance between your right to be involved parents and your doctor's medical expertise. Be mindful of being flexible.

Here are some questions you can ponder over (but feel absolutely free to include more if you prefer):

- How would you want emergencies to be handled if your partner is unconscious? Would there be freedom for the doctors, or would you require they take consent before proceeding with anything?
- How would you like the pain medication to be administered? Would your partner like it to be given beforehand or when she asks for it?
- Would you want to be in the delivery room? This is important because some dads may feel very anxious about watching their partner in pain or may not prefer being in the delivery room for other reasons. On the other hand, your partner may want you to stay for support. Having an open conversation about this can help you both understand each other and make a

collective decision.

- Would your partner like to/be allowed to move around during different stages of labor?
- Would you record or take photographs of your baby being born?
- Would your partner want continuous monitoring during labor or only when necessary?
- What would your partner think about using methods to speed up the delivery, like suction or forceps?
- What about episiotomy? This is a minor procedure where the doctor makes a small cut in the perineum to allow for easy delivery in case your partner's vagina does not stretch enough. Although some doctors make a preventive cut, not all do. Your partner should know as much as possible about episiotomies and have a say in whether she wants it or not, except in emergencies, when the doctor would take a call.
- What are you and your partner's views on C-section, cord-cutting, and skin-to-skin contact? During a C-section, would you be allowed to remain with your partner or asked to leave the room? Who will cut the cord, and what will happen immediately after birth? Will the nurse take the baby for cleaning, or will there be immediate skin-to-skin contact and breastfeeding?

The next thing you will want to think about is a doula. Doulas are not medical professionals per se, but they are fantastic for providing emotional support to pregnant women and their partners during labor. They are generally trained extensively in stages of labor, which makes them beneficial from the point of view of shortening the length of labor.

Thinking About Work-Life Balance

As a father-to-be, you can think about this from a short and long-term perspective. In the short term, you can figure out how to make more time to be around your partner for important tasks like medical visits, birthing classes, or celebratory milestones. But, as you imagine a future after the baby arrives, the changes will be more substantial and you may need to make long-term adjustments to be a present father.

You would likely want to look into your employer's policies about paternity leaves and general philosophy toward work-life balance. This will give you the information needed to start a conversation about your changing needs in the near future. This will also give you and your company enough time to adjust and collaborate on finding a system that accommodates both your needs as well as the company's. Initiating a conversation well in advance will also allow you enough time to look for alternatives if things take an unexpected turn. The idea is to keep an open mind and remain flexible.

Navigating the Third Trimester

Chances are you and your partner are feeling the anxiousness and excitement of becoming parents with a renewed intensity now. Her body will change to accommodate your growing baby, and her hormonal fluctuations will affect her mood. You, too, will go through phases of being overwhelmed and uncertain. But regular, open, and honest conversations can ease your fears and help you both see that you're in this together.

Know What and What Not to Say

Remember how the first trimester brought nausea and weird cravings to the surface? The same can continue now, and if it so happens that she throws up, try not to retort instinctively with an "Ew, that's disgusting." Or, if she wants to eat some weird combination of food items that makes you want to hurl, avoid highlighting that unusualness. Basically, be mindful of what you say to her throughout the pregnancy but more so in the final three months.

Your partner may already be feeling under-confident or insecure with the way her body is changing in the third trimester. Avoid making her conscious about the way she looks, especially if it has a chance of making her feel unattractive and unwanted. Bring in all the empathy and love you have, and make her absorb that like a sponge in water! Bring her lilies if that works.

While talking about the labor and delivery phase, it is again very normal for her to wonder about the pain and discomfort. You might even express your disbelief over how someone can go through that much pain (it can happen while you're in the labor room with her too). But, remember, if you dwell on the pain aspect more, negative thoughts can create a tense environment. While understanding and acknowledging the painful aspect is important, try to gently steer the conversation toward the happiness that awaits you both. You get the idea.

Many topics of conversation will pop up where you or anyone else will not have a straight answer, and you may not always be feeling your confident self, either. Remember then that voicing your concerns is important, but it is also equally crucial to end your conversations on an earnest and hopeful note. For example, "Honey, I don't have all the answers just now, but we will figure it out together." See the difference that your tone makes. All reassurance can be returned to a conversation by choosing the right words and genuinely expressing care and affection.

Comfort, Comfort, and More Comfort

There will be times when your partner may not be sleeping well throughout the night, and you will be by her side, letting go of your sleep as well. It can get overwhelming for both of you very quickly, and for you, it can mean lower productivity at work.

Because of the growing baby, movement will become quite restricted for your partner. Even a simple bathroom run can become uncomfortable. Getting up, sitting down, and everything we take for granted can become a difficult task. Be there for her as much as possible when you're at home and assist her with her movements.

Additionally, you can research for and invest in products specially manufactured for pregnancy. For example, a comfortable pregnancy or U-shaped pillow for your partner can provide the required support to her body as she rests, and they're snuggly!

Sex Life Can Take a Backseat: It's Okay

While the second trimester is good in terms of physical and sexual intimacy, the third trimester can slow things down understandably. Your partner may not feel up to it when it comes to sex, or her bodily changes may make sex less appealing. If it's the latter, tell her she is beautiful the way she is and that you appreciate her.

Beyond that, your partner may also feel uncomfortable while having sex because many positions become challenging to perform with the growing baby and pelvic congestion. She can also feel concerned about orgasms leading to early uterine contractions.

It's important to remember that this is all right. Intimacy can be found in many different forms, and talking about each other's needs with mutual respect can ensure that the two of you are on the same page! Even if sex is minimal or nil, being closer physically, like cuddling, can raise the bar of intimacy and be a fulfilling experience.

Now that the preparations are all done, let's turn our attention to the big day: the day of your baby's arrival.

CHAPTER 3
THE BIRTH EXPERIENCE

Sara and Josh were welcoming their first child into the world when Sarah, after 12 long hours, became really exhausted. She was in the second stage of labor, which demands even more than the first one since now is when the mom has to start actively pushing the baby. But, Sarah felt that she was done.

Her doctor was worried about her passing out, unable to continue pushing. Immediately, he asked Josh to be with her. Josh held her hand and encouraged her to hold on a little longer. He reassured her that she was doing fine and that they would have their little cuddly bundle of joy with them in a few moments. He encouraged her to breathe and reminded her of the rhythmic pattern they learned in their childbirth education classes. His emotional support worked, and Sarah mustered up enough strength to go on and give birth to their baby.

Both of them had discussed at length who would cut the cord after the baby was born, and it was Josh. After what had just happened, Josh felt a renewed sense of connection and involvement in the whole process. As he proceeded to cut the cord and gaze at their baby, his world shifted and he fell in love like never before. Both Sarah and Josh connected to one another and their baby on a whole different level at that moment.

Josh was able to handle himself and the stress of being in a delivery room calmly because he had attended all the training and prep classes with his wife as he wanted to be part of the birth experience. So, what happens when D-Day arrives? Let's unpack.

THE D-DAY: STAGES OF LABOR, DELIVERY, AND MORE

You have navigated all three trimesters with care and are waiting for the big day to arrive. You have spent days and months imagining the moment. You have visualized how it will happen. Before that actually happens, it's essential to understand the labor and delivery process.

Getting Delivery Ready

By the ninth month, you will have a checklist of essential items ready with you for the delivery time. Your preparations will take two directions. First, all the essentials you will need in the hospital while labor takes place. Second, all the essentials you will require when the baby comes home with you. As we discussed in the first chapter, you will prepare the home for your baby's arrival.

Here are the things you will need to focus on:

- Baby basics like diapers, baby clothes, swaddle blankets, a breast pump for your partner if needed, formula, and medicines, among other things.
- Nesting projects like baby-proofing your home, preparing a nursery, building a crib, or buying one, decorating your baby's room, buying toys and cuddly plushies.

You will also most likely be discussing baby names and have one ready by the time your partner goes into labor. It is also okay to have the best of two or three names with you to decide upon later once you see your baby for the first time.

Additionally, have the following things ready for the big day when you finally go to the hospital for delivery:

- An infant safety seat in your car
- A hospital bag with overnight essentials like comfortable clothes and an extra set to change into for the next day, toiletries, pillows and cushions for extra comfort, a pair of nursing bras for your partner, and a pair of shorts/swimwear (in case your wife enters a pool to ease the labor process and wants you with her)
- Electronic essentials like chargers for you and your partner's phones, or a camera (batteries too) if you want the birthing process to be documented

- Something to soothe your partner and create a comfortable environment, like music playlists or books to read to her
- Light snacks and food items because labor can last for hours
- List of important contacts, including ambulances, healthcare providers, friends, and family
- Preloaded GPS route for the hospital in your phone (memorize it if possible so you can avoid any last-minute hassles)

Know the Difference Between False and Actual Labor

In the previous chapter, we came across the concept of the Braxton-Hicks contractions, which can happen from the second trimester onward. They are irregular contractions that can feel like cramping or tightening in the uterus and are quite unpredictable. Still, they can confuse first-time parents as they are often also known as "false labor." There are a few valuable markers to distinguish actual labor and false labor.

Braxton-Hicks doesn't have a pattern and doesn't get consistently stronger. Usually, moving around or changing your position allows for them to subside. The pain is mostly felt in the front of the belly, and no other symptoms of actual labor are present. These contractions don't necessarily mean that labor will start; it just means that your body is getting ready for it to happen eventually.

In contrast, actual labor comes with its own identifiable symptoms. The two most important identifiable signals are the amniotic sac's breaking (water breaking) and the contractions' regularity and intensity. When the amniotic sac breaks, many women feel the amniotic liquid gushing out of their vagina, which is a sure sign of the beginning of laboring. Labor contractions can begin within 12 hours of your partner's water breaking, but sometimes, contractions can start before the actual water breaking. However, remember that every pregnancy is different, and it is not a rigid rule that your partner will necessarily experience her water breaking as only 10% of women experience it (Iftikhar, 2020).

The second symptom, the contractions in actual labor, are consistent, rhythmic, and keep getting stronger in intensity to the point that it may become difficult to move or talk through them. Learning how to properly observe and time them can be a nifty trick to figure out when you need to go to the hospital. Real labor contractions last for 30 to 90 seconds, don't subside with walking or moving around, keep coming regularly, and the pain is felt in the lower back, cervix, and lower belly (Cleveland Clinic, 2022).

When to Go to the Hospital

The labor process is divided into three main stages, which we will look at in detail in the next section, but it is important to know that the first stage is slow and takes time. It is when your partner's cervix will dilate up to six centimeters, and it can take up to nine hours to go from four to six centimeters. The labor pains will be felt with moderate intensity and may not be as regular. A good indicator of when to go to the hospital is to follow the 5-1-1 rule, where you have been having contractions every five minutes, lasting for at least a minute, and have been having them for at least an hour (Iftikhar, 2020).

Now, it is also true that babies love to give surprises, and we've discussed how every pregnancy can be different. Labor times can also be different. Besides, there can be many things that you may want to be cautious about in case your partner's pregnancy is high-risk or has certain complications. In that case, it is always a good practice to keep your healthcare provider's contact on the emergency speed dial and proceed to the hospital if anything unusual occurs or if you feel worried and your partner is nearing her due date. It cannot be stressed enough that it is alright to always side with caution!

Stages of Labor

The process of giving birth happens in three main stages, also known as the three stages of labor. At 37 weeks, your baby is considered full-term, and any delivery before that is a preterm delivery. Preterm delivery can happen for a variety of reasons, but the odds of survival improve as long as the baby stays in the uterus past the 24-week mark.

In the weeks before actual labor, your partner's body prepares for labor. The cervix becomes softer and thinner, the pelvic muscles relax, and the baby moves lower into the pelvic area. The amniotic sac may also rupture during early labor or at a more advanced stage when more regular contractions begin. Let's look at the stages of labor to understand how your little one will make the journey into this world.

Stage One: Making Way for the Baby

The first stage of labor involves two sub-stages: early and active labor. This is the time when your partner begins to have regular contractions closer together, leading up to dilating or opening up of her cervix and relaxing her pelvic muscles. Think of it as making the way for your baby to pass from the cervix (the uterine opening) and through the vagina. This is also the longest stage time-wise.

The early stage lasts till your partner's cervix is 6 centimeters dilated and may take anywhere from hours to days, especially in the case of first-time moms. The contractions are uncomfortable but not as intense as the active stage of labor. Doctors may intervene to ease the process if there are complications or the labor slows down after this stage.

The active stage is when your partner's cervix goes from 6 centimeters to a full 10 centimeters. The baby travels through the birth canal after the full dilation takes place. This is a more difficult stage, as the cramping and contractions become more powerful. Your partner may start feeling extreme discomfort and nausea. She may also start feeling pressure down in her pelvic zone as the baby drops down and gets ready to come out. Usually, this is when you should head to the hospital.

This is also where certain aspects of your birth plan will come into play, like the prior decision regarding when to administer the pain medication (or to have an unmedicated birth). Your partner may want to try out a few things to ease her discomfort during this labor phase, such as a warm shower, gentle massages between contractions, and rolling on a birthing ball.

Stage Two: The Baby's Arrival

The second stage of labor begins after your partner's cervix is 10 centimeters dilated. Now is the time your partner will deliver the baby. The baby's head may be visible, known as crowning, and the doctor will advise her to start pushing. They may also encourage her to follow her natural rhythm and push the baby when the urge to push occurs.

In a standard vaginal delivery, the baby's head comes out first, followed by the shoulders and the rest of the body. This stage can last anywhere from a few minutes to a few hours, depending on factors like first-time pregnancy and the administration of an epidural (Mayo Clinic, 2022a).

During the pushing phase, your partner may try a variety of positions, like squatting or kneeling. It is important for her and her healthcare providers to work together to find what works best for her. At times, mothers can be tired as they've labored for quite some time, and they can be assisted via the use of forceps and vacuum extraction. You may have discussed this while making your birth plan.

Once the baby is delivered, the umbilical cord is cut. Instead of immediately cutting the cord, a delay of a few minutes can sometimes be observed as that allows an increased blood flow from the placenta to the baby, which is rich in nutrients and oxygen, promoting the baby's overall health (Mayo Clinic, 2022a).

Many dads decide to be part of the cutting process as a way to be involved in the delivery process. If you feel comfortable and have visualized it as part of your birth plan, now will be the time the doctor will ask you to cut the cord.

Immediately after birth, skin-to-skin contact between the mom and baby is recommended as soon as possible. There are a number of benefits of skin-to-skin contact for both the mother (father as well) and the baby: it helps parents bond with the baby, calms the baby by regulating their heart rate and breathing, and stimulates breastfeeding, among other benefits like improving immunity by introducing mother's friendly bacteria to baby's skin (UNICEF, 2023).

Stage Three: Delivering the Placenta

The last stage of labor is when the placenta is delivered, usually lasting for 15-30 minutes. Your partner can still feel mild and less painful contractions, aiding the process of pushing the placenta out. Once the placenta is delivered, your partner's uterus will continue to contract to return to its usual size.

By this time, you and your partner's attention will completely shift to the baby. Congratulations, you're a father now. Savor every bit of this feeling; there is nothing like it!

DAD-TO-BE DURING LABOR

If you think that labor is essentially a mom-to-be and doctor dynamic with a minimal role for you, think again!

Your partner is actually counting on you in the most pivotal moments of her pregnancy for emotional and physical support, despite all the well-trained professionals surrounding her. The thing to realize is that, while all those professionals are specifically trained to be in that room and you're not, you still matter the most in the context of emotional bonding and comfort. Your support will count the most in encouraging her through the different stages of labor.

Advocating for Her

As your partner moves through the more difficult stages of labor, she will increasingly focus on delivering her baby and breathing through the intense pain. She will likely be unable to think about anything else, including your mutual decisions and preferences about the birth plan.

You can be her advocate! Even if a doula is present to advocate for her, personally communicating your partner's needs and preferences can have a crucial impact on them being respected and cared for. Of course, you are not expected to replace medical advice in any manner, but your partner's wishes about things, such as pain medication or other medical interventions, can undoubtedly be relayed to her healthcare providers.

Additionally, if she falls unconscious during any stage, you will be the one giving consent to the necessary/emergency medical response needed at the time. Therefore, you play a fundamentally important role here, and keeping yourself updated on the situation will enable you to support your partner better.

Physical and Emotional Support

Labor can be an unimaginably painful experience before the moment of unbound joy of holding your baby in your arms. While your partner will experience physical exhaustion, possibly fears and anxiety, and emotional burnout, you will also experience difficult emotions seeing her go through such an ordeal.

This is where your dependable-as-a-rock dad persona can kick in. Your loving reassurances, telling her to breathe through the contractions, and words of encouragement and appreciation can make her experience much better and comparatively relaxed. Phrases like "You're doing phenomenal," "You're doing great for our baby," and "You can do this," can go a long way to fortify her resolve to face the labor pains.

During the early stages of labor, you can massage her lower back (or wherever she asks you to) or feed her ice chips (she will not be allowed to eat anything once she is in the hospital and progressing to advanced stages of labor anyway), make conversation to distract her from the pain, or pretty much anything that she requires. Once the second stage begins, she may be unable to keep up any conversation with you and less likely to voice her needs. In that stage, make sure you are around her and attentive. Even if there are moments that she ends up snapping, show the utmost kindness you can because this is extremely difficult for her.

You can also gently caress her forehead or wipe her brows with a cold towel to comfort her during intense moments. Express your love to her for all that she is able to do in that moment.

Creating a Comfortable Environment

Hospitals can be scary places with troubling atmospheres. They're also unfamiliar places. You can take small steps to create a more comfortable environment and bring some familiarity to the delivery room. For example, you can bring a playlist with the kind of music your partner enjoys and play it at a low volume to create a relaxed ambiance, or have some of her favorite fragrances in the room (ones she does not have an aversion to!).

Comfort can also mean reading a book to her, watching something together in the early stages of labor, taking care of light snacks, and, most importantly, hydration! Keep water around you to offer her at different points during the process.

Documenting the Birth of Your Baby

While memories can fade over time, photographs are an important reminder of magical moments. Since your partner will mostly be remembering the agony of childbirth, you need to be the one documenting the whole thing to enjoy with her later.

If you both have discussed this and she is comfortable, take lots of pictures and videos. Even if they are unflattering, they will become a treasure trove to be cherished. You can also take weird selfies that you both can laugh at later. Definitely take lots of photos of your newborn baby in his jelly-blob look!

Informing Friends and Family

Having a baby is not just a personal celebratory event but a deeply social one too. While you can be in the hospital with your partner as she delivers your baby, many family members and friends will be eagerly awaiting the good news. You can be the conduit, share the news with all of them, as well as the enthusiasm and joy of becoming a parent.

If you have planned to host a small welcome get-together for when you take your partner and baby home from the hospital, now is the time to involve your close circle of people in the preparations and keep them updated. It is also time to let them know whether you will buy a welcome baby boy or baby girl banner!

If you stay at the hospital for a bit longer, you can coordinate visits from family and friends, keeping your partner's and baby's comfort in mind. Documenting the first time your loved ones meet your baby can be wonderful and is encouraged as well. These small things bring great joy later!

MY BABY IS BORN, NOW WHAT?

In the immediate moments after your baby is born, one of the first important tests done is the APGAR test. Introduced in 1952 by Dr. Virginia Apgar, the test takes place within one minute of birth and is then repeated after five minutes. APGAR is an acronym for Appearance, Pulse, Grimace, Activity, and Respiration. The test checks basics such as skin color, heart rate, baby's breathing, and reflexes (Rudick & Brott, 2021). It is very normal for newborn babies to appear purple or deep red after birth, but within a few minutes of blood circulation and breathing, their color normalizes into that baby pink hue.

Meanwhile, your baby's measurements, like length and weight, will be taken. He will also be wiped down to get rid of the vernix and given an ID tag or wristband. He will be wrapped in a warm blanket and then given to you or your partner to be cuddled. At times, if the baby is breathing fine, he may immediately be put to the mother's chest for skin-to-skin contact before being taken to be cleaned.

Some routine and standard immunizations will also happen in the first 24 hours after your baby is born. These two important injections are Vitamin K, which aids blood coagulation, and the Hepatitis B vaccine, which will be administered along with some antibiotic eye drops to prevent infection (Schnabolk, 2023).

If your partner tries to breastfeed the baby, you can assist her in positioning the baby or just celebrating the first milestone of your baby's first feed. Your support will be necessary here because this can be a hard step for your partner if they want to breastfeed and it's not working.

Births seldom go according to plan, and sometimes there can be certain medical complications that may require urgent care. If your baby is not breathing normally, his airways may be cleared to aid breathing. Sometimes, if the baby is born with special conditions needing special care or is born prematurely, he may be taken to the neonatal intensive care unit (NICU).

While all this happens to your baby, your partner will also undergo specific changes. Physically, her body will slowly return to its original state of being but with certain changes. She will continue to have contractions, which will ease in a few days. There will be discomfort when she uses the bathroom and more so if she has received an episiotomy or is recovering from stitches to repair tears. Her breasts will change and may feel swollen (engorgement) due to increased blood circulation and the presence of milk for the baby (Cleveland Clinic, 2018; Rudick & Brott, 2021).

More importantly, emotionally, your partner may go through what is called "the postpartum blues." Just as it happened during her pregnancy, a shift in her hormonal levels causes mood swings, and postpartum changes in hormonal levels can affect her emotions. She can go through sudden bouts of crying and sadness. This is a crucial time for you to support her with empathy and kindness as her body and mind are both recovering from the delivery.

Sometimes, women also go through postpartum depression. If she seems unusually sad or overcome by fear and guilt, cannot focus on everyday tasks, or no longer takes pleasure in things she normally loves, she may be suffering from this condition. It's important to have an open and reassuring conversation with her and get her professional help if needed. The idea is to allow her to acknowledge her feelings and work from there.

All things considered, now is the time to celebrate, but also set your sights on what comes next: bringing your newborn baby home and surviving that phase!

CHAPTER 4

HOW TO SURVIVE THE NEWBORN PHASE

Nathan and Sandy were proud parents of a baby girl who absolutely loved to become active and expressive at 3 a.m. After the entire day of running around, taking care of her, soothing her, and feeding her, both the parents wanted nothing more than to have a good night's sleep—if only their daughter would sleep at the most sleepable hours through the night!

Here she was, little Sophie, her eyes wide open, and Nathan groggy. It was his time to watch and care for Sophie as Sandy rested. He kept trying, in vain, to sing to his little girl so she would go to sleep. However, the more he sang, the more she found her dad amusing and stared at him wide-eyed. *Poor Nathan!* He knew he would not get any respite until Sandy woke up in the morning.

Welcome to the newborn phase, where you will love your baby so much, but your life will turn upside down. Most of your time with the baby will be divided into three parts: sleeping, feeding, and changing diapers.

While there are no strict manuals on how to do this phase right, some tips and ideas can make you bond with your baby and care for him without you and your partner being completely exhausted (even though some exhaustion is inevitable).

It's crucial that you remember parenting is a learning curve. Be patient and kind to yourself, create healthy routines, take the collaborative parenting route, and ask for help when needed, especially from close friends and family (and accept it!).

Being the best dad in the world and an involved father means taking the initiative to share tasks and supporting your partner as a fellow team member in the common goal of caring for your baby. This involves finding a balance that works for both of you in terms of sharing childcare responsibilities.

DECODING THE SLEEP PATTERN

As we saw in the first chapter, your baby's sleep patterns will be wildly different from your own, and even though newborns sleep for most of the day, they do so in small breaks of one to two hours rather than a stretch. Sometimes, you may find your baby drifting off to dreamland one moment and being super-charged the next. You get the idea!

Babies have small stomachs, so they wake up every few hours to feed, and generally, their sense of day and night is not very clear. Most babies don't start sleeping through the night until they're three months old; some don't until one year. But generally, they are up every two to three hours to have their feed.

Decoding your baby's sleeping and feeding pattern will help you understand her rhythm and mutually divide your time. Remember, the pattern is not set and continues to change rapidly as your baby grows. For example, maybe you can devise a system where you care for the baby from 8 p.m. to 2 a.m., and then your wife steps in from 2 a.m. to 8 a.m. This way, you can both get six hours of sleep at a time. When you are in charge, you can try feeding the baby with your partner's bottled breast milk without needing to wake her for it. This is to give a basic idea of how sleep time can be adjusted, and of course, you both will figure out what works best for you and your baby.

New parents often go through a period of questioning and doubt over properly caring for their baby. It's natural. Don't worry; you will get the hang of it. Be kind and remind yourself that you're doing great.

Here are a few useful tips for you and your partner to navigate this phase:

- Try creating a safe and comfortable sleep area for your baby by dimming the lights and keeping it quiet during nighttime feeding.
- You can use white noise or soothing background sound to help your baby sleep. There are many apps that can help with this.

- Put up black-out curtains to make it pitch black so your baby can start learning morning from night, and know that it's time to sleep when it is dark.
- Nap when your baby naps! This one is probably a savior when it comes to saving your energy. Getting some rest when your baby sleeps will allow you to make the most of your rest time.
- Ensure that your baby is placed on his back in the crib with a firm mattress and no loose bedding.
- Swaddling your baby correctly can ensure they feel safe and warm enough to fall asleep (which will be discussed in the next section).

Swaddling Your Baby

Swaddling is a great technique to wrap your newborn baby into a thin cloth or a blanket to keep them snug and cozy. It can be thought of as providing a similar experience of coziness from when they were in the womb. Swaddling is also said to help your baby sleep more soundly and for more extended periods. It prevents your baby's arms and legs from flailing and triggering their startle reflex, causing them to wake up (Taylor, 2023).

Here are the step-by-step instructions on how to swaddle your baby:

1. Spread the swaddle blanket flat on the bed or a flat surface with one corner pointing upward in the shape

of a diamond. Fold the top corner down for about six inches.

2. Gently place your baby on the blanket, face up, with his head above the top fold of the blanket. His legs should be straight, pointing downward.

3. Gently straighten your baby's left arm so that it is next to his body, pointing down toward his legs. Take the left side of the blanket and bring it over his body to the right side covering his chest. Tuck the blanket just beneath the right arm and back. The right arm should be free at this time.

4. Take the bottom corner of the blanket and bring it up over the baby's body to tuck it under his chin, where the left fold overlaps.

5. Now, gently straighten your baby's right arm and bring it down next to his body. Repeat the process mentioned in step three and tuck the blanket behind your baby's back on the left side.

6. Finish wrapping your baby's swaddle by twisting any remaining blanket gently and tucking it gently under your baby.

While this cute little swaddled bundle looks adorable now, you must keep a few things in mind to ensure your swaddling is safe. Remember that it should never be too tight, or your baby will not be able to move or bend her legs. Movement is important for her hip and joint development (Taylor, 2023).

Alternatively, if you don't feel comfortable with a blanket, you can look for a premade swaddle wrap with velcro or zippers attached to make your life easier and your baby's more comfy!

A note of caution: While swaddling is great for babies, not all babies like it. Some babies will try and wrestle to be free of the folds and cry relentlessly if they're unable to. It is alright if your baby does not like to be swaddled. All babies are different, and their comfort is paramount. So, keep an eye out for how your baby behaves.

Another side note on when to stop swaddling your baby: A general consensus exists that when your baby is about two months old or attempts to roll over, you should stop swaddling her as that can be dangerous. Some babies can take three to four months as well. Again, it will depend on when your baby becomes more active.

Sleep Training Your Baby

Babies don't have a very well-developed circadian rhythm that helps them fall asleep at night and wake up in the morning or any general sense of day and night. Routines and habits, repetitive activities, and consistency help establish these differences for them. This is where sleep training also comes in.

Sleep training is basically a collection of activities and techniques that help your baby sleep through the night and self-soothe if they wake up in the middle of the night so they can fall back asleep. Most babies can be ready to be sleep-trained by the time they are four to six months old. Some parents also start by the time their baby is nine months old since they don't wake up as much through the night for feeding (Suni, 2023).

There are different methods you can use to sleep-train your baby:

- **The fading method:** This is where a parent(s) stays in the room and around the baby until they fall asleep. Each night, the parent gradually moves further away to allow the baby to adjust to the distance and slowly get into the habit of falling asleep without the parent being expressly present in the room.
- **The gentle sleep training method:** This is where a parent focuses on teaching their baby to fall asleep without crying. This involves being present and following a consistent set of bedtime activities, followed in the same order, to help the baby recognize it is time to sleep. If the baby cries at any point, the parent immediately calms them and reassures them while putting them back to bed. The idea is to make your baby feel comfortable lying in bed and falling asleep on their own instead of in your arms.
- **The cry-it-out method (CIO):** This technique is a bit different and relies on the parent following a bedtime routine, like cuddling or kissing their baby, before eventually leaving the room. The parent does not immediately respond or return to the room if the baby cries and allows the baby to exhaust himself before falling asleep. However, this method is difficult for

some parents as it's hard to let your baby cry without immediately consoling him.

You can choose which training method works best for your baby and modify it according to your particular situation.

FEEDING YOUR BABY

Alright, you may be wondering, "What am I going to do here?!" Of course, the major job here is done by your partner, but that doesn't mean you have no role to play at all. Understanding what babies eat and how often can make you an empowered father who can participate in the process too. Yes, you heard that right.

Babies obviously don't eat what we do (no, you can't boil and smush veggies to feed them or give them fruit juices). Their first meal is a milky substance called the colostrum, which is produced before the mother starts producing milk for the baby a few days after delivery. This breast milk will be largely what your baby will consume for the coming months, and it contains important nutrients for immunity and health.

Your role here is to support and assist your partner through the feeding process. Breastfeeding can be an uncomfortable and painful experience for the mother, as her nipples can become raw, and her breasts can become swollen with the pressure. A good nipple cream and a breast pump to relieve the pressure and store her milk can make her breastfeeding experience more comfortable. As her breasts can often feel heavy and leak milky fluid, she will require nursing bras and extra pads for support and prevent her clothes from becoming wet.

Babies initially feed every two to three hours and gradually develop a more consistent feeding pattern. Identifying and following that pattern consistently can further help your baby recognize daytime from nighttime.

Participating in the feeding routine is one of the most important things you can assist with. After she feeds the baby on one breast you can burp him while she gets ready to feed them on the other side. You can also encourage her to pump her milk so you can feed the baby during the night while your partner rests.

SOOTHING A CRYING BABY

The relationship between your baby and crying is crucial since that is the only communication skill they have at the moment, and it's their only way to tell you they feel uncomfortable. However, a relentlessly crying baby can have you scrambling for some secret recipe to calm him down. For some parents, their crying baby can also mean they go into intense self-doubt mode and have feelings of inadequacy as parents.

Let me stop you there and ask you to take a deep breath! Babies cry, and it does not mean one bit that you are failing at your duty as a parent. Remember, just like your baby is adjusting to the world, you too are adjusting to being a parent too and will learn how to be good at it.

Having said that, it helps if you understand what are the major reasons your baby can become fussy. Knowing why your little one is crying is the beginning of learning to use the most suitable technique to calm them.

The most common reasons for babies to cry are (Geddes, 2021):

- they're hungry or tired
- their diaper is wet
- they're gassy and feel uncomfortable
- they're tired or bored
- they're feeling too hot or cold, especially since it can take some time to nail the number of layers needed to keep them at just the right temperature
- they're sick or in pain
- colic

The last one is particularly difficult to deal with and overwhelms new parents. Colic is basically prolonged or excessive crying in an otherwise healthy baby (Cleveland Clinic, 2023). Differentiating between normal crying and colic can be difficult. While the doctors are unsure what causes colic, there is a general rule that if your baby cries for more than three hours for three days over three weeks, he may suffer from colic (Geddes, 2021).

While it can take you some time to figure out why your baby is crying and which of their cries means what, some tried and tested methods can ease your baby into calming and falling asleep.

Dr. Karp (n.d.) explains the five S's for soothing crying babies:

- **Swaddling your baby:** We have already seen how swaddling can make your baby snug and warm.
- **Side or stomach position:** Holding your baby on his side or stomach over your forearm can be soothing to them.
- **Shushing:** Gently holding and shushing your baby may provide a reassuring environment for him. Babies like the vibrating sound and your touch that can mimic their time in the womb.
- **Swinging:** Gentle swinging and jiggling motions can help distract your baby and calm him down; however, be careful to properly support their head and neck, and never shake your baby, as that can be dangerous for them.
- **Sucking:** Sucking can lower a baby's heart rate and calm them into falling asleep. You can try giving your baby a pacifier or your own thumb from time to time (remember to always have clean hands when interacting with the baby or picking him up).

These are not exhaustive of what you can try to soothe your baby. You may have to use all five tricks at the same time to help calm your baby down. Now you have tips and tricks up your sleeves to get your baby out of fussy land and into happy land!

Using a baby sling to carry them around is a great way to distract and stimulate your baby's mind. Your baby is experiencing life outside the womb from a completely *tabula rasa* perspective, which means they have a clean slate. They will absorb everything with wonder in their eyes. At the same time, remember not to overstimulate them as that can have an opposite reaction.

If your baby has some gas trapped in their tummy or is constipated, you can try the gentle bicycle pump method by making her lie on her back and gently bring her knees up to her stomach for a few seconds. It can help relieve the gas and help her calm down.

You can also try singing to your baby or a gentle massage her on the back. There really is no limit to what you can try to entertain your little one. Whatever you try, remember to do it all with love and patience.

THE DIAPER MISSION

Now, this is something you definitely can help out with, and yes, it will not be pretty!

Babies can have all kinds of poop, and it's important to know how to distinguish the normal ones from weird ones. Your baby's first bowel movement is called meconium, a mixture of greenish-black tar-looking substance that includes amniotic fluid, mucous, and bile, among other things. It is sticky in texture and can stay around for two or three days before more normal-looking poop arrives.

Eventually, the poop turns to brownish and yellowish tones with the consistency of thick paste or curry, depending a large part on whether they consume breast milk or baby formula (Swanson, 2023). It also changes with time as your baby eventually shifts to semi-solids and solids.

A note of caution: Although any tone ranging from greenish, yellowish, and brownish is normal for babies, do keep a lookout for black or red poo because that can be a sign of fresh bleeding due to constipation (red streaky poo) or internal bleeding (black poo). Further, a gray poop can indicate that your baby's liver is not producing enough bile to break down and digest food. Contact your doctor immediately in these cases.

If your baby passes watery thin poop with mucus streaks, and it's happening more frequently than your baby's usual, it may be a sign of diarrhea. Diarrhea can be caused by milk allergies, certain viral infections, antibiotics, or too much fruit juice. Take care to keep them well hydrated; if there are signs of dehydration like sunken eyes or dry lips, call your doctor immediately (Swanson, 2023).

With that out of the way, let's come to the basics of diaper changing. If you take the initiative with this, your partner will love it, and you will get an interesting opportunity to care for and bond with your baby. Here are the things you will need:

- a changing table
- changing sheets
- clean diapers (you'll go through more packs than you expected!)
- diaper cream to prevent or heal rashes
- baby wipes

- disposable bags or a diaper genie

Follow these simple steps to change your baby's diaper like a pro:

- Wash and dry your hands, and get your supplies ready and in front of you at arm's length so you don't have to look for them when your baby is in all his naked glory.
- Spread a changing sheet on your changing table so that if the baby goes during the changing process, your table does not get dirty. Gently lay your baby on his back on the changing table and unfasten the dirty diaper from the sides. Then, raise your baby's bottom by holding their ankles together gently and raising them upward.
- Slide the diaper from under them and keep it away from the baby. Don't go on throwing away the diaper just now. Never leave your baby unattended or away from your sight, certainly not while he is on the changing table.
- Clean your baby's bottom and genitals with the baby wipes gently. Remember that your baby's skin is very tender at this point, and sometimes they can get a rash.
- If you have a baby boy, clean thoroughly around the penis and scrotum. To avoid getting a pee fountain on you, make sure to keep a clean diaper or cloth over the penis. If you have a baby girl, always remember to wipe from front to back to avoid infections. Only clean the external areas of any poo or pee debris (Brown, 2022).
- Baby girls can have some vaginal discharge that is white or blood-stained, which is normal in the first two

weeks. But if it persists beyond that or has a strong odor, you should consult your doctor. Keep a check on your baby for any unusual odor, color, or consistency in their poop or urine.

- After cleaning, you can apply a rash ointment or moisturizing cream to their bottom and air out their diaper region for a few minutes before putting on a clean diaper.
- Put on the clean diaper by first sliding it under your baby's bottom. Remember that the attaching tabs should be under your baby's bottom side, not on their abdomen, or you will find it difficult to stick them. Many diapers come with identifying markings to distinguish the front and back.
- Secure the diaper safely by bringing it between your baby's legs and over the stomach and attaching the tabs on the side. Remember to point the penis of your baby boy downward to prevent him from peeing outside the diaper and on himself.
- Ensure that the diaper is snug but not too tight or loose.
- Finish up by rolling up the soiled diaper and throwing it away safely, then wash your hands.

See! It wasn't so difficult, was it? Now that you are a pro at diaper changing, it's time for you to get all snuggly with your baby and make some memories.

BONDING WITH YOUR BABY

You love your baby from the second he arrives in this world, but you are also getting to know this new little human. All human relationships take time to grow, and this beautiful one between you and your baby is no different.

You can do a lot to acquaint yourself with your child and slowly fall deeper in love with him. Spending as much time with your newborn as possible benefits the baby and you. Research shows that the more time you spend holding your baby, the more you release oxytocin, which is the love hormone responsible for forging bonds (Gettler et al., 2021).

The documenting journey does not stop after delivery. You can continue to record your baby's growth. One of the most fun things to do is to record your baby's antics, their laughter, and how they behave throughout the day. While newborns don't do much specifically, you can catch glimpses of their awesome baby-ness, which is sure to melt your heart in the future as well.

Celebrating milestones is a sure way to make you feel a part of your baby's journey. For example, you can privately celebrate your baby's monthly birthdays or have a small get-together with your friends and family. It brings you closer to your baby, creating a stronger family unit. You can share pictures on your social media or with your loved ones privately, whatever works for you. The first time your baby rolls over, crawls, or tries to walk, stands up, or walks are all precious moments not to be missed. You and your partner can record video messages for your baby as they cross important milestones, which will be shown when your baby is all grown up, like their 18th birthday!

You can even create a memory wall in your home, which is regularly updated as your baby grows and captures all such milestone moments. Additionally, you can buy meaningful gifts for your baby, like a storybook or a toy they respond to and enjoy playing with.

Take the initiative to soothe your baby when he cries, and try the different techniques discussed above. This will also make you confident as a father who can care for his baby and make your baby understand that he can rely on you for comfort and reassurance. This feeling of connection is very important in parent-child bonding.

As your baby grows, you and your partner may realize you have many converging and diverging approaches to upbringing. And, even though you may have had those conversations before, when your baby actually arrives, these similarities and differences can become more stark. How do you handle when there is a serious disagreement about what's best for your baby? Let's focus on this in the next chapter, which will discuss navigating roles and responsibilities.

THE FIRST TIME DAD SURVIVAL GUIDE

Simple Tips for Expectant Fathers to Confidently Support Their Partner During Pregnancy and Parenthood to Become the World's Best Dad

Dear New Father,

Congratulations! You're about to embark on an incredible journey as an expectant father and Harmony Brooks "The First Time dad Survival Guide" is here to be your compass through the magical adventure of pregnancy and parenthood.

A MAGICAL TALE UNFOLDING

Imagine this: after 9 months of watching your partner struggle, with hormone changes and physical changes it's time to meet your beautiful baby. Nothing can prepare you for that incredible moment of seeing that babe and snuggling it for the first time. What a magical moment that's your and yours only.

SIMPLE TIPS FOR EXTRAORDINARY MOMENTS

This book is filled with simple yet powerful tips for expectant fathers like you. It's a guide that goes beyond the technicalities of parenthood, delving into the emotional and transformative experience of becoming a dad.

RELATABLE STORIES, PRACTICAL ADVICE

"The First Time Dad Survival Guide" shares relatable stories and provides practical advice that will resonate with you. From managing the fear of seeing your partner in pain to the sheer astonishment of witnessing the miragle of birth, this book covers it all. It's a heartfelt exploration of the million thoughts that rush through a father's mind, silenced by the over-whelming love that washes over him as he holds his baby for the first time.

YOUR INVIATATION TO SHARE

Now we invite you to share your thoughts on this extraordinary guide for expectant fathers. Your review will not only help other dads-to-be but will aslo contribute to the shared journey of fatherhood.

Here is a link you can click on that will let you leave a review.

If you prefer here is a QR code you can scan:

Thank you for considering sharing your thoughts on "The First Time Dad Survival Guide." Your review is very much appreciated. Especially for all the other new fathers out there that would love a survival guide. If you know a father that is expecting be sure to share this book with them!

Wishing you an incredible journey ahead!

Warm regards,

Harmony Brooks

CHAPTER 5
NAVIGATING ROLES AND RESPONSIBILITIES

Fatherhood has undergone an enormous change in the present times as a social and personal experience. No longer is traditional upbringing seen as the mother's job, with the father being a disciplinarian or "breadwinner" figure. Today, you will find that all kinds of fathers want to be involved in childcare in various settings.

Once your baby is home, you and your partner will encounter many new challenges on a daily basis. While some days it will be easier for you to manage and navigate through different concerns, some days will appear extra hard when you feel your patience is being tested. Because you want to be an involved dad, learning to resolve any differences is key to creating a loving environment for your family.

Here, we will discuss four essential aspects of being a father you can be mindful of to become the best dad for your baby and strengthen your relationship with your partner. These four things are:

- understanding your role
- stereotypes of fatherhood
- open communication for effective co-parenting
- nurturing your relationship with your partner

Let's look at these aspects one by one.

UNDERSTANDING YOUR ROLE

Within the changed dynamics of your family, your role is now akin to an anchor. You have an essential responsibility to be a good dad to your kid and an emotional pillar of support to your partner. Yes, you are still her friend, lover, and partner in life, but she will rely on you the most while she recovers from the delivery of your baby and beyond that. As a father, you are not only your wife's life partner but also a partner in parenting or, as they say, a co-parent.

To that end, be realistic about your expectations of returning to your pre-pregnancy schedule. While you wonderfully supported your wife through the nine months of pregnancy, you are now entering a different phase of support. Any last-minute emergencies with the baby, such as doctor visits when he falls sick and vaccination visits, among other things, will call for you to be present.

Your education, learning, and research will not stop. You did all the reading when it came to understanding the stages of pregnancy and labor, but now that journey will continue further in terms of proper nutrition for your baby, building healthy habits, and interacting and playing with your baby for their proper behavioral, mental, and emotional development. Research shows that fathers' involvement with their children plays an important role in their mental health, emotional regulation, being socially well-adjusted, and performance in school (Lansford, 2021). So, play with your child, read to him, and explore the world with him as much as possible. When your child starts growing and talking coherently, answer all the weird questions he throws at you. Or better yet, get involved and help him look for an answer!

As you encourage your child to learn about the world around them, you must cultivate a lot of patience within yourself. Having an open and flexible mindset and curiosity to learn every day will help you adjust your expectations and be responsive to your baby's and partner's needs.

STEREOTYPES OF FATHERHOOD YOU MUST BUST

As you move along the path to fatherhood, dispelling certain myths and stereotypes associated with what it means to be a dad and their roles is a foundational learning experience. We have all grown up with preconceived notions about how dads should be. Stereotypes, in general, are harmful, but more so when it comes to parenting. Some stereotypes especially related to fathers are particularly damaging.

Dads Are Important as Breadwinners Only

Fathering starts from the time of pregnancy itself. The development of your baby is dependent on the environment in which your partner is living. A stress-free and supportive environment requires much more than just money (we will see that later). Fathers play a crucial role in providing that positive environment in many ways, ranging from healthy lifestyle habits to caring for the pregnant partner and ensuring her rest.

Further, as Linda Nielsen (2023) informs us in her book, *Myths and Lies About Dads: How They Hurt Us All,* having a rich dad does not automatically mean well-balanced, emotionally stable, and happy children. Though money increases the probability of a child's needs being met, that alone doesn't mean anything if fathers are not actively engaged with their children.

Research also shows how the new generation is already busting the myths of overworked and/or absent fathers (Jezard, 2018). Chances are that if you are reading this book, you already don't believe in this stereotype, as you have made the decision to be a more engaged dad—and that matters.

Maternal Instinct Outweighs Paternal Instinct

This one is perhaps the single most harmful, misinformed opinion to have ever existed in the world of parenting. While this myth has many socio-economic causes, let's look at what the science says about this supposed gender divide in parenting.

As Nielsen (2023) explains, instinct denotes automatic behavior like fear. It is not learned. Instead, parenting and caring for children is something that every parent grows into. Many first-time mothers feel overwhelmed, confused, afraid, and anxious about properly taking care of their babies, which is why they turn to educational resources like books and the internet or seek help through nannies. Mothering is also a social skill learned over time, and every mother-child dynamic is different. Caregivers evolve in relation to how their child responds to and engages with their caring.

Calling motherhood instinctive implies that fathers cannot compete with the natural talent that women are born with, which is not the case. If proper caregiving is learned, both parents can learn it. Fathers who engage with their children contribute more significantly toward ensuring a balanced home environment and mentally and emotionally healthy children (Neilsen, 2023).

But, what about the science? One reason the motherhood instinct is projected as natural is the hormonal changes women undergo when pregnant and after the baby arrives. Oxytocin is known to be the hormone responsible for bonding between humans in general, mother and child in particular. Research shows that fathers also go through similar changes, and the level of oxytocin also increases in men as they become dads and engage with their children. The human brain is malleable, and caregiving experiences transform neural networks in the brains of parents (Abraham et al., 2014; Neilsen, 2023).

Dad's brains *are* the caregiver's brains!

The Contradictory Tough Dad-Clown Dad Myth

In different times, various images of the father have dominated our society. On the one hand, an image is conjured up to show a tough, disciplinarian kind of father who is incapable of showing tenderness and emotion. He is also depicted as over-worked and absent. On the other hand, dads are represented as the clowns in the family who are least concerned with home matters and only care about fun. Both images are being broken by the present generation of fathers who take a greater interest in balancing their responsibilities and engaging with their children lovingly and meaningfully.

As you may have figured by now, you have the power to decide what kind of dad you want to be! Navigating through these stereotypes is not easy. It calls for you to be mindful of them when you encounter them.

OPEN COMMUNICATION FOR EFFECTIVE CO-PARENTING

Discussing different parenting approaches can sometimes bring up conflicts between you and your partner. It is important to understand that no one's viewpoints are necessarily right or wrong; they are just different. Different can mean good. Different approaches only add to your child getting the best of both worlds, a richer tapestry of learning from both of you.

However, if you cannot resolve conflicts constructively, you may end up disturbing your child. Even though your munchkin is just a newborn without much understanding about the world, he will eventually grow up and start picking up verbal and non-verbal cues inside and outside the home. It is well known that frequent and aggressive conflict between parents can negatively affect children, making them anxious, fearful, and sad. It can also lead to various other health problems like sleep disturbances. The situation becomes even more serious if the disagreements are about the child (Sutherland, 2014).

Therefore, knowing how to keep communication channels open to constructively and calmly resolve conflicts while establishing a solid co-parenting relationship with your partner is paramount.

Voice Your Concerns Respectfully

Discuss your concerns and parenting styles with your partner as openly and respectfully as possible. Oftentimes, things can be easily discussed if we become mindful of our tone. Along with that, our body language says a lot. Verbal and non-verbal cues hold immense importance for the quality of conversations we have with the people around us.

It is understandable that with the pressure of caring for a newborn and the exhaustion that comes as a result of sleep deprivation, we can lose our minds at times and feel extremely overwhelmed. However, cultivating patience and mindfulness goes a long way in helping us voice our disagreements without sounding like we are blaming someone.

Always try to speak about your experiences while leaving space for the other person to contribute as well. Use sentences with "I" in them to focus on and highlight your experience, ideas, or opinions, as this can avoid sounding like you are aggressive or blaming your partner. For example, let's say you have a disagreement about how to best sleep-train your baby. You can say, *"Honey, I think we should try this particular method because it is known to be more beneficial for babies, but let me know your thoughts so we can talk about it."*

At the same time, ask open-ended questions to seek clarification from your partner about things. This does not constrain the conversation to the limits set by you and allows your partner to bring in their opinions and thoughts to a situation.

Active Listening

Another important thing to include in your conversations is active listening. It means you don't just hear the words someone is speaking but try to understand them with a genuine interest. It involves having empathy and the ability to put yourself in the other person's shoes while you think from their perspective.

Try to look for solutions to resolve disagreements and conflicts constructively. This means understanding each other's perspective with an open mind and, most importantly, not interrupting each other while speaking. Let the other person finish their point and never dismiss them. Remember that you are on the same team as your partner, and your goal is the same: caring for your baby in the best possible way. Keeping this common goal in mind can help you look at the bigger picture when things become frustrating or overwhelming.

In addition, patiently allow your partner to listen to you and reflect before responding. Trying to pressure anyone into giving an answer to a question or responding to a situation is not the best way to seek common ground.

Acknowledge and Validate

When your partner expresses something, acknowledge and validate her experience. Reassure her too. This is quite important to avoid miscommunication and hurt feelings. Sometimes, we can become defensive and miss the point of an open conversation.

Pregnancy is a challenging time physically, as well as emotionally, for your partner. While you also go through many ups and downs, your partner's body literally goes through painful changes. The hormonal rush does not make things easier. The postpartum experience is also difficult for mothers to adjust to. In such an emotionally charged situation, you have to act like the anchor we talked about a little while ago. Your role is to provide emotional support and stability to your partner as she heals and adjusts to the reality of being a new mom.

This does not mean you won't feel overwhelmed or frustrated. Realistically, you will feel all that way at times. But, this is where patience becomes the key. When things become too hot with a chance of becoming aggressive, a good strategy is to take some time off. You can inform your partner and leave the room physically until you calm yourself and are ready to continue the conversation.

On the other hand, share your own feelings and vulnerabilities with her. This will bring you closer and allow your partner to see you in a very humane light. It will give you an opportunity to feel supported and heard too. This mutual support works wonders to bring couples closer.

Timing Is Everything

While conversation is important, always know when to initiate that conversation. Timing is everything.

Suppose you can see your partner is already agitated about something or is barely functioning due to exhaustion. In that case, it's not a good idea to invite her to a dense and possibly serious conversation. Alternatively, if you feel emotionally overcharged or slightly annoyed, avoid getting into any discussion, as there are chances that you will end up saying something that you don't mean.

The best time to have a conversation is when you both are relaxed and on the same wavelength. Disagreements can be easily sorted through when you both have the same emotional bandwidth to hear each other without taking things personally.

Additionally, take care and respect your partner's privacy. Never discuss your disagreements in front of others who can do more harm with their unsolicited advice or create more friction by seemingly siding with you or your partner. Of course, asking for help from friends and family is great. They can be a support system, but they can't replace the mutual understanding and relationship you and your partner have as co-parents. Therefore, always be mindful of having difficult conversations privately.

Meeting Each Other Halfway

Being a team means striking a balance and mutually reaching a compromise when things get difficult. Using positive and affirmative language goes a long way in achieving this, as our words carry weight.

Always use solution-oriented language and sentences that are positively affirmative instead of highlighting and dwelling on issues. If you display your willingness to work through problems, you display your commitment to the whole situation and your support for your partner. Meeting her halfway is sure to encourage her to do the same.

Appreciation and Gratitude

Lastly, conversations are not only for voicing unpalatable feelings and thoughts in a constructive manner. They are also to express appreciation and gratitude.

Imagine what your life would be like if your partner and baby were to vanish from your life. Sometimes, an inverted perspective helps us value what we have and reminds us not to take some of the most beautiful things in our lives for granted. Once you see what your partner and baby add to your life, absorb it and acknowledge it. Appreciate it. Show gratitude for your partner's efforts and willingness to communicate openly and without judgment.

Ask follow-up questions and check in with each other regularly. Asking for feedback shows your openness to improve the situation and working to improve things. It creates a positive loop in your partner's mind and will reassure her anytime she wants to share something. It is a strong sign of a healthy and secure environment you help build. That is a pretty cool dad thing to do!

NURTURING YOUR RELATIONSHIP WITH YOUR PARTNER

Chances are that you haven't had sex with your partner since the last months of the third trimester, and you are eager to go back to that form of intimacy. However, your wife cannot have vaginal sex for at least four to six weeks after delivery. If she is breastfeeding, her sex drive can decrease further (Holland, 2019).

However, that doesn't mean you can't nurture other forms of relationships with your partner. Physical and emotional intimacy after delivery can renew your bonds, and here are a few ways in which you can do this:

- **Prioritize quality time with your partner so it's just you two reconnecting with each other.** Plan date nights, dinners, or outings to spend time with your partner. You can ask a family member to care for the baby during that time.
- **Find other ways to be intimate.** Indulge in other ways of showing physical affection, like cuddling.

- **Plan surprise gestures for her, like a sweet love note or a small meaningful gift to remind her how much you love her.** You can even encourage and plan self-care days for both of you together or just her if she needs her "me time."
- **Plan big decisions together.** After the baby arrives, you become cemented as a family unit. Involving your partner in all small and big family decisions, creating daily rituals together, or planning trips and getaways will bring you closer as equal partners.
- **Encourage and support her passions.** Share her dreams. Share yours too. Share your common dreams as parents as well. Pregnancy can leave your partner with a lot of doubts about getting her individuality or professional career back on track. Make sure you show her that she can have it all and that you will stand by her in whatever she chooses.
- **Show each other respect.** Allow and respect each others' space to be in solitude and have time outs when needed.
- **Seek professional help like therapy or couples counseling if the need arises.** Don't shy away from exploring all available options to strengthen your relationship jointly.

The crux of your relationship post-pregnancy will depend on how well you manage to juggle different roles and responsibilities of being a partner *and* a father, in addition to being your own person. But, with the big picture in mind, some patience, and a whole lot of love and understanding, you will sail over the difficult tides. Sure, it will not be very easy, but all of it is worth it when you get to be the coolest dad around the block!

But, wait a second. Even cool dads must care for themselves because being a dad is a full-time and exhausting job. Unless you focus on your self-care, you cannot be a supportive father or even a happy human. So, turn the page and look at some interesting facts and tips on self-care for dads in the next chapter!

CHAPTER 6
SELF-CARE FOR DADS

Let's start with the "why" of self-care. *Why* is self-care important for new dads, especially first-time dads like yourself? In fact, *why* is self-care essential for anyone at all?

The act of taking care of your physical, mental, and emotional well-being is counted as self-care, and it is indispensable for living a meaningful, authentic, and fulfilling life. If you think about the history of human evolution and invention, everything we have done and achieved as a species has centered around bringing that fulfillment and satisfaction to our lives.

Self-care is the most basic requirement to fulfill our potential in the world. Framed in this way, can you now tell me *why* self-care is important for dads? Yes, you're right. If you want to be an effectively involved dad, you must bring your best foot forward every day. You cannot do that if you function at half your capacity. Therefore, you must embrace self-care practices without guilt or shame—not only for yourself but also for your family. You deserve it!

While parenting will make some form of exhaustion inevitable, burnout is certainly avoidable. But for that, recognizing some common signs of parental burnout is important. These include having brain fog and confusion, forgetfulness, being short-tempered, feeling isolated, depression, increased stress, and sleep deprivation, among other serious health symptoms that put you at risk for heart disease and diabetes (WebMD, 2023).

THE IMPORTANCE OF SELF-CARE FOR DADS

Caring for your physical, mental, and emotional health makes you a better father and more equipped to deal with the challenges of fatherhood. It allows you to be responsive to your child's needs and be an attentive and present father.

In fact, indulging in self-care routines is a healthy habit that your child can learn from. You can be a cool role model, Dad. Seeing parents take care of their well-being teaches the child to prioritize self-care as they grow up. This means they become attuned to their needs and better regulate themselves emotionally.

Self-care can benefit you as a father in innumerable ways, such as (WebMD, 2023):

- It reduces stress levels and anxiety to better cope with the demands of parenting.

- It also enhances focus so you can be involved fully with your child and make better decisions to benefit your personal and professional life. It also leads to better problem-solving skills.
- You can nurture healthy relationships when you are in a good headspace and emotionally balanced.
- Your sense of well-being is holistically taken care of when you give yourself the time for self-care activities.
- Self-care is closely linked to a sense of personal identity and your self-esteem as it reminds you of the importance of fulfilling your needs. It reinforces your value in your mind.
- It has long-term health benefits, as reduced stress levels are linked to better physical and mental health.
- It allows you to better balance your roles as a father and partner.

How can you incorporate self-care activities into your routine when you are so occupied with your responsibilities? It doesn't have to be something very difficult or complicated. You can take simple steps to find time, unwind, and care for your soul.

FINDING YOUR "ME TIME"

Finding the time for yourself is crucial for your mental and emotional health and is also linked to overall physical health (WebMD, 2023). This section discusses some self-care strategies you can try to adopt or modify to suit your needs.

Setting and Communicating Your Boundaries

The first step toward your self-care is an honest conversation with your partner. We have already seen in the last chapter that proper communication is the foundation for a healthy and strong relationship. As part of that communication, you must also communicate your boundaries and needs to your partner.

Nurturing a supportive relationship is always a two-way street. Just as you respect your partner's space and boundaries, she must understand yours. Taking the initiative to be vulnerable and expecting your needs to be met is also part of being equal partners. So, go ahead, have that talk with her, and protect your boundaries, especially if you feel emotionally overwhelmed.

Pursuing Interests and Hobbies That Fulfill You

Hobbies and interests are synonymous with self-care activities. They nourish your soul and recharge your batteries when you're down or low. Take time out for that one thing you love a lot, be it cooking, painting, or even fitness or sports. Workouts are a great way to rejuvenate yourself. Form a relationship with that task or hobby and watch as it transforms your life by giving it a richer and broader meaning. Cultivating any hobby is a great way to unwind.

Becoming a parent puts things that you usually enjoy on the back burner. Finding a way back to those things can restore some sense of self-identity to you, especially if you have been struggling with it after the baby arrives. It's alright to acknowledge it without any guilt because your life undergoes a profound change, and everything becomes about the baby.

However, that does not have to mean you lose yourself completely because that would hinder your quality of life and your aspiration to be an involved and loving father. So, take your time to connect with the things that make you feel alive and see their positive effect on your life as a dad.

Do the Basics

Self-care absolutely does not have to be some big fancy-schmancy thing. Little things that we do every day that don't require planning can be converted into an act of mindful self-care.

The next time you go for a shower, think of how it relaxes you. Stand under the showerhead and feel the trickle of water running down your spine and relaxing you. Visualize all your exhaustion and stress being washed away as you emerge rein-vigorated.

Similar activities can become part of a simple self-care routine for you, like getting a massage or walking in the park. Being in nature is wonderful for your mood and overall well-being. Connecting with nature is a powerful, calming, and grounding experience. It's even better if you live near the ocean or a body of water. Go out, look at the waves, and be hypnotized by their rumbling or the gentle lapping sounds of water in a lake.

If you're a musical kinda guy, make that a part of your self-care. Listen to relaxing ambient music or any style that stirs your soul. Feel the instruments and beats. Focus on how it makes you feel and how your breath syncs with the music's highs and lows.

The idea is to inculcate mindful awareness in your day in whatever you do so that you gain some sense of conscious living instead of living on autopilot. Keep an open mind and try out different things. Before you know it, you will find your rhythm.

Planning Ahead of Time

Your self-care activities can be planned in advance. It is always good to put it down directly in your calendar so that you can adjust your schedule accordingly and prioritize your self-care by committing to it—just like you would commit to any other task in your calendar.

Such planning is good for activities like travel. Traveling to a new place or a different one, even if not new, is an excellent form of self-care as it gives you a much-needed change of environment. It can stimulate your mind from the boredom of routine and refresh your senses. So, go ahead and plan that trip!

Involving Your Baby in Your Self-Care

What could be more wonderful than involving your baby in your self-care activities? It would be a fantastic opportunity to re-energize yourself while bonding and spending time with your baby. One way in which you can achieve this is by taking your baby with you on a nature walk. Alternatively, you can establish a calming bedtime routine for your baby that allows you some evening free time afterward.

Another way is to involve your baby indirectly! Yes, you heard that correctly. What I am suggesting is that you can utilize your baby's nap time for some self-care. You can choose to take a power nap at that time or any other activity that relaxes you. But, remember to choose something calming and relaxing because, as a father to a newborn, exhaustion will be your biggest challenge to face.

Limit Your Screen Time

Research has shown links between screen time and mental health. The more time you devote to screens, the higher your chances of having low mood and depression incidents. Screen time before bed is also known to disrupt sleep patterns by inhibiting melatonin production (Mayer, 2020).

While in our technological world, screens are unavoidable, you can take small steps to ensure it does not become an additional source of stress for you. Therefore, be mindful of your time with screens and be sure to avoid any before bedtime.

Avoid Over Committing

This point connects very well with the first point of setting boundaries. Increased responsibilities at home and juggling work can eat into your personal time. Allow yourself to manage your time in a way that leaves enough for you to prioritize your self-care activities.

Whether at work or at home, delegate tasks to colleagues, friends, and family to free up your time. Remember, asking for help does not make you a failed father but one who values his health and understands the connection between his well-being and being present for his loved ones.

At work, utilize your breaks wisely. In those breaks, choose to recharge yourself and power through instead of indulging in work-related activities like checking and responding to work emails.

Combine Your Self-Care With Family Time

Just as you can combine your self-care routine with your baby time, you can also involve your partner and family in your self-care. You can involve them in a new hobby or undertake some creative activities together that help you do something constructive with them and allow you to unwind. Family and friends are excellent support systems and they can show up for you in surprising ways.

For example, playing old board games, card games, or a good old-fashioned game of charades is a fantastic way to bond and relax with family. You get the idea! Explore and let your creativity run wild here.

Create Your Space and Incorporate Mindfulness

Having time and space dedicated to your self-care is a great way to solidify your habit of taking compulsory timeouts for yourself. You can designate a specific space within your home that is only yours and where you can incorporate activities centered around bringing more mindfulness to your life.

This space can be used for you to engage in multiple exercises like the 5-4-3-2-1 grounding technique, which is very helpful in reducing stress and anxiety. It is a great way of getting back to your body by engaging your senses. It involves identifying five things you can see, four things you can touch or feel, three things you can hear, two things you can smell, and one thing you can taste.

Activities focusing on movement are also good for getting centered and shaking off stress. You can also follow guided meditation videos to connect with your inner self and bring more calmness to your life. Depending on what works for you, you can either do this early in the morning, before your day starts or wind down before you go to sleep.

A SUPPORT SYSTEM OF OTHER DADS

Having a strong support system translates into a feeling of belongingness. While your family and friends can certainly be very supportive, not all of them will have had the experience of being a father.

You can look for and join support groups for fathers or parenting communities. Connecting with other dads across the board can bring valuable insight into your parenting experience and answer many questions. Being part of a mutually supportive group of dads can help you in your journey.

Connecting with like-minded individuals from diverse walks of life is always a good idea. They provide an interesting opportunity to diversify your own interests and network with people who can open new doors of self-care for you. For example, you can join a sports or hobby club, or even attend local networking and business events that offer a chance to connect with dads.

Connecting with fathers from different areas of life can bring various aspects of fatherhood to light for you. Take a work-from-home dad, for example. He can have flexible schedules and be more available for playdates for your kid.

Initiating conversation and bonding with dads who are also going through similar experiences at your workplace can offer mutual help. It can also be beneficial from the point of view of office policy since all involved dads can initiate a conversation about how your place of employment can best support working fathers (bonding has practical benefits that way!).

With that, we come to an important aspect to keep in mind. Self-care has two dimensions. One is personal, your "me time." The other is professional and social, where you relate with other people. The next chapter discusses how to strike that balance between your work and family life, which is also an important part of your self-care because both areas of your life are indispensable to leading a fulfilling life as an individual, a partner, and a cool dad!

CHAPTER 7
BALANCING WORK AND FAMILY

You have already thought about this one. You want to be the pillar of strength your family deserves. And, sometimes, that comes with a set of hilarious situations. Or, at least, it's funny in retrospect, like it was for Steve.

Steve was a work-from-home dad with a 10-month-old baby. There he was, caring for his son, when an unscheduled but important work meeting was set up. With his wife out to get groceries, it was up to him to do the balancing act! Just as he joined the call, with his baby in his lap, his laptop perched up perfectly on his desk, he prayed with all his might that his baby would remain his usual calm and happy self. The meeting went smoothly for the most part before little Sam decided it was time to let everyone know of his presence! As Steve addressed his colleagues, Sam looked up at his dad's chin and, for reasons only known to him, laughed his cute little person laugh—almost as if he saw something really funny on his dad's face.

While Steve was embarrassed about losing his train of thought, he was absolutely not sorry and enjoyed the moment, as did his colleagues.

Research has shown that children with involved fathers are more likely to be well-adjusted behaviorally, emotionally, psychologically, socially, and cognitively. It has also shown that fathers who are involved in bringing up their children live happier and fuller lives. Overall, companies that are considerate and provide benefits like paternal leave and flexible time to balance work and family perform better in terms of employee satisfaction and productivity levels (Behson & Robbins, 2016).

The Covid-19 pandemic further changed how we work. In many ways, it allowed us time to reflect on what we prioritized as important. One of the changes it brought was the increased number of dads wanting to continue work arrangements that allowed them to be present at home with their kids (Miller, 2023).

Whatever the case, transitioning back to work from parental leave or taking a different work path can be tricky. Visualize the kind of father you would want to be. Of course, you will feel simultaneous pulls and pushes in different directions. Don't worry though; you will get through that too. All you will need is a bit of planning and foresight.

UNDERSTANDING THE NEW WORK-LIFE DYNAMIC

The changed dynamic of your work and family life will require you to strike a delicate balance. It starts with negotiating flexible work arrangements and prioritizing tasks so that you have more time for your family.

At the same time, knowing that a perfect balance is not always achievable is equally important. The idea is to modify things and build a system that best suits you and your unique needs. Work and family life are unpredictable, and you should be prepared to remain flexible and adapt to situations, as well as respond creatively to challenges and opportunities.

Ideally, it would appear that our work should stop when we are out of the office and at home, and vice versa. However, that is not how life works. Most of the time, both of these aspects will bleed into each other, and you'll be juggling both things.

So, how can you ensure you devote adequate time to your work while not compromising your family time? The following sections discuss some possible ways you can explore to achieve that balance.

When at Work

Firstly, the best way to initiate changes in your professional life is by discussing your life as a dad in your workplace. Start a conversation around the theme of being a dad at work and how it has diversified your responsibilities and priorities. You may find people who relate to your experiences and go through a similar journey of balancing work and family life. There may even be people who may have wanted to be involved with their own children but could not due to work constraints. The idea is to create a space for such discussions to occur if they aren't already taking place or if your workplace does not offer that space. This can build a feedback loop where your experiences can help create a sense of unity around seeking a proper work-life balance.

As we saw above, responsive companies fare better regarding employee satisfaction and productivity levels. In fact, fathers who utilize paternity leave feel more satisfied with work when they do return, and the positive effect spills into their work and family (Glassdoor, 2022). You can leverage this understanding and negotiate flexible work arrangements to accommodate your parenting responsibilities.

Once you initiate the conversation, clearly communicate your needs and priorities to your employer and establish certain boundaries. Yes, I know you probably think this is easier said than done! But, it may not be as difficult as it seems. With changing times, employers and workplaces have generally evolved to incorporate flexible working styles. Well-being is becoming an indispensable part of work culture. Being sensitive to employees' different needs and commitments is a great way to ensure their overall well-being is being taken care of.

Discuss the possibility of remote work as part of your negotiation for a flexible working style. Many companies provide the option of working from home a few days a week. Such arrangements can help you, especially if your partner is also considering returning to work. It can help your savings as you will not have to hire a nanny or a babysitter every working day of the week. More importantly, it can give you the much-needed time to bond with your child at home and be present for important milestone moments.

While you are at work, delegate the tasks that your fellow colleagues can effectively handle. We often get caught up in the trap of productivity and perfectionism. We also forget to ask for help. Realizing the need to conserve your energy by not exhausting yourself entirely at your workplace is a huge step toward striking a healthy work-family balance. If you're exhausted, whatever time you do get with your family will not be as meaningful as when you are fully present. So, ask for help and accept it when necessary.

In a similar vein, avoid overcommitting to work-related tasks. Anything that has the potential to keep you at work for more than the expected amount of time and possibly upset your work-family balance should be avoided as much as possible. Of course, life happens! Work will throw up unpredictable circumstances, but managing them will become an important aspect of juggling work and family. Be kind and understanding toward yourself if there are commitments you absolutely cannot get out of, but ensure that you do mindfully consider and discern the times when you can delegate work and when you cannot.

There are many other ways to ensure you engage your office time productively. Things such as getting organized using calendars, to-do lists, and task boards can do a neat trick here. It's no surprise that with so much riding on your shoulders, along with the responsibility of caring for your baby and supporting your partner, there will be times of confusion and overwhelm.

Having something to organize your daily or weekly tasks as you see fit will be a huge help. Not only can they help at your workplace, but they can also be nifty while planning family activities.

Finally, make sure you take short breaks in your workday to maintain your energy and prevent burnout. Research shows that periodically pausing your work to take short breaks positively impacts your well-being and increases your productivity while boosting your performance (Lyubykh & Gulseren, 2023).

When at Home

When you are at home with your partner and child, ensure that you offer your undivided attention to them. Being fully present with them is the best way to support them and bond with your family after your baby has arrived.

Disconnect with your work, and if need be, keep a limited time dedicated to work-related tasks if complete disconnection is not possible. Prioritize your time around your family and tasks related to childcare. Your baby's formative years need attention from both you and your partner.

It is important to dedicate time for special activities with your family, such as having meals together, planning outings or picnics, or even trips, and playing with your baby. The idea here is to carve out some non-negotiables for your family time. For example, some families consciously decide to have at least one meal of the day together. Some have movie nights every week on a specifically dedicated day. The more time you spend doing different activities together, the richer your connection with your family will be. In the initial months after your baby arrives, making your own little family rituals will set the foundation for the future.

Devoting your time at home to family does not mean you will have no space for yourself. As we saw in the previous chapter, self-care rituals and your "me time" are just as important as spending time with your family. So, when you are at home, be mindful to allocate some time to your self-care and hobbies that make you reconnect with your sense of self.

The pressures from juggling responsibilities often make you feel you have no option but to pull overtime at home too. But, remember that is not a healthy approach and is bound to affect your quality of life and relationships in the long run. Therefore, resting is paramount and should also be prioritized. Make sure to be well-rested, form a workout routine to keep you active and healthy, and remember to meet your nutritional requirements.

Lastly, as discussed in the previous section, work commitments are sometimes difficult to avoid. In that case, communicate your work expectations openly with your partner and figure out how to manage the situation like a team. There will be times when you will compromise and other times when your partner will. That is where prioritizing your family commitments can make it easier to collaborate.

There will occasionally still be times when you and your partner will be in a tight spot. Regularly assessing your work-life balance and asking for feedback from your partner will go a long way when it comes to readjusting your time and focus.

Words of reassurance and encouragement can bridge the gap you may feel while balancing work pressure and family responsibilities. So, remember to appreciate your partner for being there and standing with you in this, and be kind to yourself for doing your best.

QUALITY VERSUS QUANTITY TIME

Involved parenting means spending quality time with your child. Always make the most of your time with your child and engage him in different stimulating activities. These activities are about bonding and setting a strong foundation for your child to appear confident and emotionally well-balanced in the world.

When you try to engage your child, you are also teaching your child numerous valuable lessons. Parents are the first people that children forge a relationship with. In the earliest days, it is a relationship of complete dependence as your baby is helpless and relies on you for comfort and soothing, physically and emotionally.

As they grow up, their observation of your actions and behavior becomes a role model for them in regard to how their future relationships with their fellow peers will be patterned. Children who grow up in a secure household with healthy relationships with their parents have a much better chance to experience fulfilling relationships later in life. They also learn to self-regulate better and deal with stressful situations by developing healthy coping mechanisms (Parenting NI, 2018).

Here are some qualitative ways to spend your time with your child:

- **Always make sure to put them to bed lovingly and kiss them goodnight.** This can make them feel secure from a young age before sleeping and reassure them that daddy is there no matter what.
- **Make rules and boundaries to teach them the value of having a structured and disciplined life.** Use positive reinforcement techniques instead of harsh punishments.
- **Fun is as important as rules.** Play with them lovingly and inculcate values like team spirit and grace while winning or losing.
- **Play mentally stimulating games like puzzles and riddles with them.** You could also engage in learning activities with them like quizzes.
- **Be an active and empathetic listener to your child.** Always give them your undivided attention when they share something and match their enthusiasm even if you are exhausted. This goes a long way in making your child feel valued.
- **Make time for adventure.** Take your child out for hikes, nature walks, or amusement parks and do something fun together.
- **Encourage their hobbies.** If your child shows a predisposition toward art, paint with them. You could sing and dance with them.

- **Never show harsh judgments if they are learning something.** Harsh judgments can make them shut down or not try something they are not immediately good at. Always encourage them to try new things.
- **Teach them resilience with kindness.** Scolding or yelling does not do the trick.
- **Don't force them to do anything they feel uncomfortable with on the pretext of making them "tough" for the world.** That only alienates your child.
- **Talk it out.** Have heart-to-heart conversations with your child and create a safe environment for them to be able to share anything with you.

The possibilities are endless. You can even draw from your own childhood and play games or plan activities that you loved as a child. Wear your creative dad hat and let the magic flow!

ACHIEVING WORK-LIFE INTEGRATION

Alas, you have managed everything but life will still throw up challenges. Remember that the approach to striking a work-life balance cannot rest on a complete separation between the two. Sometimes, they will overstep each other's boundaries. A different way of looking at this is to think in terms of work-life integration.

Work-life integration is a more holistic concept that rests on combining the two areas of your professional and personal life to create a synergy rather than seeing them as conflictual or mutually opposing. The approach centers on flexibility, creating meaningful boundaries, and innovative benefits to the employee (Hirsch, 2023).

It's no secret that we live in a technologically driven society. This technology can be leveraged to achieve work-life integration, where you carve out greater autonomy for yourself and choose how to be productive. For example, with the Covid-19 pandemic, the physical office shifted to a virtual office. Many companies adopted platforms that allowed real collaborative work to happen in a virtual setting. With different software solutions, such as online meeting platforms like Zoom or Google Workspace, to collaborative projects online, there is no shortage of creative innovation.

While these decisions may majorly depend on your company and the kind of work you do, there are still some things you can do to achieve a greater work-life integration (Wooll, 2022):

- Transform your understanding of productivity and let go of the trap of perfectionism. Allowing yourself some space is crucial to maximizing your productivity.
- Allow for flexibility and adaptability. Keeping a flexible schedule allows you to respond to any emergencies or day-to-day requirements of your family more effectively.
- Planning ahead of schedule on how to manage personal and professional tasks so you can have enough time for other activities as well as rest and rejuvenation.
- Bring more authenticity and well-being to your life and understand that work is important but only one aspect of your life, not your entire life.

With technology, you can also take steps to connect with your family during work. During breaks, go on a quick call with your partner, see your baby, or drop in to check how things are going. Once you get the hang of it, achieving an integrated work-life balance will become easier and lead to fulfillment on both professional and personal fronts.

Now that you are equipped with the tools to balance your work and family life, let's turn our attention to another aspect of fatherhood: safety. As you bring your baby home and witness his journey of turning into a toddler and young child, giving them a safe environment will become your major focus.

CHAPTER 8
NAVIGATING SAFETY CONCERNS

You would be surprised to know that babies and toddlers can be at risk in your home from the most mundane and unassuming things. For example, one of the most common safety hazards for your kid can be your furniture. Toddlers are fond of crawling into the weirdest places possible and hurting themselves. Or, they can climb onto stools, chairs, or stairs and accidentally fall. Hot liquids, sharp objects, and even small toy particles can pose a threat of choking to your child if you don't have them under your supervision.

But what about your home as a whole? How can you ensure that your house is baby-proofed? The preparation can start from the moment you know your partner is pregnant. While you educate yourself on childbirth and the stages of pregnancy, you will also be educating yourself on safety concerns.

Providing a safe environment also means focusing on the physical and mental well-being of your family. Let's look at both aspects one by one.

GETTING YOUR HOUSE READY FOR THE BABY

Preparing your house for the baby can be overwhelming. If you break down the process into smaller steps, you can systematically safeguard your living space. Following these tips on baby-proofing your home can help you set up well in advance and save time for when the baby arrives (Geddes, 2022):

- Keep your house up to date with renovations and ensure no hazardous materials are lying around. This includes covering all electrical outlets, storing cords and wires out of reach, and sharp objects away from easy access.
- Heavy furniture, like the television, bookshelves, and dressers, should be appropriately wall-mounted to prevent accidental tipping. Use covers for the sharp corners of your furniture.
- Install window guards.
- Keep a first-aid kit ready with all essential supplies like antiseptic wipes, bandages, medicated ointments, and medication.
- Use childproof locks or latches in bathrooms and the kitchen for cabinets containing potentially hazardous chemicals, like cleaning supplies, or sharp objects like knives, heavy pots, and pans. Children like exploring,

and if they have access to these objects anywhere inside the home, they could harm themselves.

- Keep matchsticks or lighters for burners away from your child's reach.
- Always keep dishes and containers containing liquids away from the edges of your table to avoid your child accidentally knocking them over. This is especially important if you use a tablecloth, as your child can pull on its edges and yank it down.
- Protect your gas burners with knob covers so they don't accidentally turn them on.
- Always watch for small objects, like toy pieces, that could be a potential choking hazard for your kid, and select only age-appropriate toys.
- Keep a check on carbon monoxide and smoke detectors, and make sure they are fully functional. Install them near all sleeping areas and appliances using fuel.
- Remember to install the toilet seat lock to prevent your child from accidentally lifting the lid unsupervised. Keep cosmetic items stored in locked cupboards.
- Never leave your child unsupervised around water, whether in a bathtub or the inflatable kiddie pool, and make sure to empty the buckets after use to prevent accidental drowning.
- Take care of the water temperature (ideally, 98.6-100° Fahrenheit or between 37-38° Celsius) while bathing your baby to avoid any accidental burning.
- Throw away any unused or expired products, medicines, and food items.

- If you have plants in your home, make sure they are non-toxic and out of reach of children so they don't accidentally break the leaves and try to eat them!

PREPARING YOUR BABY'S NURSERY

This is the most important room to take care of since this is where your baby will spend the most vulnerable time of their day: their sleeping time. Read on to find out how best to set your baby's crib for a safe, good night's sleep (Lascurain, 2020):

- Keep the crib simple with no loose bedding, sheets, or comforter lying around. Don't place stuffed toys in the crib.
- Blankets and bumpers pose a risk of suffocation to the baby, so avoid them.
- Keep a well-fitted, water-resistant sheet in the crib with a firm mattress. The mattress should be well-fitting too, with no gaps between it and the frame.
- The crib posts should be high enough to prevent their clothes from getting caught up in them.
- The crib's sides should be fixed as movable sides pose a risk to your baby, especially when they become more active.
- Don't hang anything over the crib that contains long strings, as they can pose a strangulation hazard. All heavy items, like mirrors or large frames, should be avoided as they can accidentally fall, causing an injury to your baby.

- Regularly inspect the crib and ensure it is always in the best condition. Any damage of any sort should mean an immediate change.
- Don't place the crib near a heat source; position it away from direct sunlight, as babies can overheat.
- The height of the mattress should be adjusted as your baby grows and starts to roll over or crawl to prevent him from accidentally climbing over and falling.
- Always keep electronics, even the baby monitor, at a safe distance from the crib and never in it.

Now that your home is baby-ready, it's time to look at the second aspect of providing a safe environment for your baby: ensuring the physical and mental well-being of your family. A healthy family is key to a healthy environment for a child to grow. Only when you and your partner take care of yourself can you both care for the baby effectively.

A HOLISTICALLY SAFE ENVIRONMENT: PRIORITIZING WELL-BEING

Providing a safe environment goes beyond the mere physical. It encapsulates your entire being. Caring for a baby is a full-time job that will take precedence over everything else in your life. This means that you will have to take extra care and be mindful of not neglecting other areas in your life. Everything you do to manage different responsibilities and cope with stress levels will create an example for your child to emulate.

Think of this as a holistic approach to safety: a balanced life. Here are a few quick tips to focus on to ensure that you and your family's physical and mental health don't lose its much-deserved focus:

Physical Dimension

- Give ample thought to leading a healthy lifestyle and encourage your family to do the same.
- Establishing healthy routines will help your baby to also be mindful of health from an early age and go a long way in building his resilience.
- Incorporate a fitness routine in your day and choose any activity you like, whether it's swimming, jogging, yoga, or a sport. Physical activity is known to promote feel-good hormones in addition to known benefits for your health.
- Eat well. A balanced diet rich in fruits, veggies, lean protein, whole grains, and healthy fats will provide you with all the required nutrients for optimal body functioning.
- Stay hydrated. Water intake is often overlooked by us when living through stressful situations but it is the only miracle drink you absolutely need to have during happy hours!
- Get a healthy seven to nine hours of quality sleep every night and maintain that schedule. Taking care of your circadian rhythm is very important as it regulates a lot of other bodily functions. Proper sleep helps maintain weight, improves concentration, keeps your heart healthy, and keeps your immune system healthy (Leech, 2023).

- Limit screen time and avoid it completely, if possible, before bed. While relying on technology is unavoidable in today's time, we can be conscious of our use of it.
- Schedule regular health checkups for yourself and your family to monitor your health.

Mental and Emotional Dimensions

- Mindfully incorporate stress-relief techniques in your family's routine, like meditating or deep breathing.
- While you focus on your self-care, promote your partner's self-care too. She may need your active encouragement and loving reminders to take care of her soul too amidst the enormous responsibility of childcare.
- Take time for heart-to-heart communication with your partner and share your feelings and vulnerabilities. Rely on your friends and family for emotional support and seek out support groups if that works for you.
- Be a support system for your child. Children rely on their parents in their formative years for emotional security, and you can build a supportive environment for your child by being present, emotionally available, and responsive to their needs.
- If you experience prolonged feelings of anxiety, depression, and overwhelm, don't be afraid to seek out a mental health professional. Remember, mental health matters and affects all parts of your life. Help is available and you deserve it!

- Always be kind to yourself and set realistic expectations of being a good father. Perfection is a myth and we all do the best we can. Include positive self-talk and encourage yourself to believe that you are doing well.
- Positive affirmations upon waking up or before bed can help you reorient your thoughts.
- Journal your feelings. Acknowledge and validate them, sit with them, and process them. Repressing what we really feel is exhausting and detrimental to our self-esteem.
- Remember that effective time management means taking time to rest and for self-care. There is nothing called failure, only lessons.
- Set personal goals and celebrate them as, and when, you achieve them. However, be mindful not to beat yourself up if you fall short. Goals are there to guide you through your day, week, or month, but life happens. Rigidity will not allow you to flow and adapt to changing needs and circumstances around you. So, let go of fixed expectations and allow yourself to breathe.
- At the end of the day, love and support can heal you from the most difficult of experiences. Give love, but also learn to accept it.

STAYING INFORMED AND INCLUSIVE

Finally, a safe environment can mean staying an informed dad and advocating for your child's interests in different settings. It also means imparting inclusive values to your child as they learn to navigate the world and helping them identify what is acceptable and what is not.

Informed Parenting

The cornerstone of informed parenting is staying updated and having an attitude of wanting to learn all there is to learn about how best to raise your child. An involved and conscious parent will research and educate themselves on effective parenting styles and ways of establishing a nurturing relationship with their child.

While there is not one correct way to raise your child, there are research-backed findings that show which way is comparatively better and beneficial for the holistic development of your child.

Researchers identify four main parenting styles: authoritarian, authoritative, permissive, and uninvolved (Morin, 2022). You may have experienced one or more of them in your own childhood, or you may have certain ideas on how to raise your child that may fall into either of the categories. Being aware of them and their impact can help you make a conscious parenting choice. Each of these styles can be identified by certain core beliefs on how best to raise children.

Authoritarian parenting is premised on the belief that children should follow the rules without any exception or question because the parent knows what is best for them. Usually, when disciplining the child, parents don't give any reasoning or justification as to why something should not be done, and often, children's opinions or feelings are not taken into account. This style also comes with stress on harsh disciplining tactics like punishing children instead of focusing on teaching the child to make better choices. Sometimes, parents with such an approach can become hostile and aggressive. It can negatively affect children as they may feel fearful of sharing their opinions or feelings with their parent(s), uncomfortable and insecure about their experiences being rejected, and possibly grow up to have a tendency to lie.

Authoritative parenting, on the other hand, differs from the above approach. It is important to keep in mind the subtle difference in the spelling of this word, but the big difference in the approach it has toward parenting. This style is characterized by building and maintaining a positive relationship with your child in terms of rule setting, enforcing, and consequences. Parents take the time to explain to their kids why certain rules exist. They also balance their approach by giving their children the space to ask questions, share their feelings, and feel heard. Children's feelings are validated, but, at the same time, a clear boundary is established, namely, that the adults are in charge. Positive reinforcement strategies are also used, like utilizing a reward system and praising children when they behave well. This parenting style is considered to be the most balanced one, with an overall positive impact on kids as they grow up to be happy and responsible adults who feel comfortable advocating for themselves and expressing their opinions freely. They may also make better decisions in life and self-evaluate risks.

Permissive parenting is characterized by the rarity of setting rules and enforcing them. Parents believe that their children can learn with minimal interference from them and may play the role of being a friend rather than a parent. They also don't enforce consequences regularly and may forgive their child too easily or give back privileges to them if they throw a tantrum or plead. This form of forgiveness can quickly turn into coddling, where parents don't discourage their child's poor choices or bad behavior effectively. This approach can negatively impact children as they can grow up with a dislike for rules and authority and may even have behavioral and health problems because of an inability to develop healthy habits.

Lastly, *uninvolved parenting*, as the name suggests, involves parents being uninvolved in their child's life intentionally or unintentionally. Parents can be neglectful toward their child due to any reason, ranging from addictions and substance abuse to mental health issues. There is no guidance or nurturing relationship present here, and children end up raising themselves since their needs are not met and little to no attention is received from their primary caretakers. Uninvolved parents usually have no idea what their child is doing or what type of company they keep, and they don't take out or are unable to take the time to ask about basic things like their day at school or homework. A child growing up with uninvolved parents may feel disconnected, depressed, and encounter behavioral problems (Morrin, 2022).

Parenting styles are not absolute and can overlap at different times. Conscious parenting on your and your partner's part will require both of you to have a conversation about your parenting styles and common goals. Choose mindfully which approach to take and when to change it because these have a lifelong impact on what kind of person your child will grow up to be.

Having said that, it is also important to realize that this is a huge responsibility and there is no manual on how to do it best. *That is exactly why it is a crucial practice to stay informed and updated about parenting research and guidelines.* Evaluating your parenting style is also a good practice.

Advocating for Your Child's Well-Being

Being informed will allow you to support and advocate for your child effectively in different settings. Every parent wants their young one to grow in a safe and enabling environment to achieve their full potential. Sometimes, that can mean promoting and defending your child's interests in places like their school or going the extra mile to get them the guidance and attention they need if they struggle with something.

For example, suppose your kid faces learning difficulties or mental health issues or needs other forms of special assistance. In that case, you will be their foremost source of active support and take the initiative to fulfill their needs. Let's see five powerful ways in which you can effectively advocate for your child.

Firstly, knowing your child's rights will give you the much-needed foundation to defend their interests. Educate yourself as much as you can on the different laws and regulations meant to promote and protect children in your region (Katz, 2022).

Secondly, communicate your child's needs proactively with the adults and peers present in and around your child's life. For example, if your kid requires special assistance in school, be open and engaging about it with the teachers involved in her education. Of course, first, you need to know your child's needs, observe them, and listen to them actively and patiently. Also, ask questions to gain clarity, as kids may not always know how to express their needs. It is important to provide them with a safe space so they can open up and engage with you.

Thirdly, get professional help if needed. This involves legal services as well as counseling, therapy, or mental health services if your kid needs them. If your child has health concerns, getting doctors on board can provide your case with much credibility in trying to advocate for their interests.

Fourthly, build a support system for yourself in the parenting community by being part of parents' associations, support groups, or advocacy groups that work for children. This kind of community support not only helps in putting forward your child's concerns more effectively but also provides important emotional solidarity in times of difficulty. Remember, there is strength in numbers!

Lastly, be persistent in your efforts and keep hope. Advocacy for your children is important but also emotionally overwhelming at times, especially if you and your child face resistance or challenges from others in the peer groups, whether adults or children. It is also important that you support your child and empower them to not be afraid of taking a stand for themselves as they grow into a young adult.

Teaching Diversity and Inclusion

Finally, as an involved dad, you will want to impart value on education to your child so they grow up to be responsible and good people, contributing meaningfully to the society they live in.

As our world becomes increasingly interconnected and we move toward acknowledging and respecting the diversity of human communities and experiences, you must ensure that your child learns the important lessons of inclusivity. It will help them understand the world with kindness and acceptance and make them a socially conscious individual when they grow up.

How can you do this? It starts with unlearning your own biases. Here too, educating yourself and being open to different ideas around diversity will enable you to create a more accepting environment in your home. Keep an open mind and read (or watch and listen) as much diverse literature as possible on different people, different cultures, their struggles, and triumphs.

The next step would be to involve your child in the process. Openly and honestly communicate with them as and when your child observes diversity around them and comes up with curious questions. For example, maybe at school or on the playground, your child may interact with and ask about children from different social, economic, racial, and cultural backgrounds. Answer all questions they have with patience and teach them to respect everyone for who they are.

You can also take care of putting your child in diverse groups while they play, learn an activity, or pick up a hobby. The best way to teach respect for diversity and inclusion is to allow your kid to play and interact with a diverse group of kids. It can truly open your child's mind and bring home the important lesson of equality and respect for all humans.

With this, you are on your way to becoming the best dad who is going to raise the best kid as they encourage and inspire the world!

CHAPTER 9
BECOMING THE WORLD'S BEST DAD

Now that we are at the end of our journey, all there is left to do is see how you transform into the world's best dad. Being the best dad is not really about how many books you read about fatherhood. At the end of the day, it's about being there for your child, forging a nurturing bond where he feels safe and comforted while learning how to survive in the world and live meaningfully. In a way, it's also about preparing your little angel for a life after you. It is about passing all your knowledge and the traditions you have grown up with throughout your life to your child.

Let me tell you about Peter and his children. Peter's dad started a tradition of having a small treasure hunt every Saturday night for him and his two other siblings. In his memory, the game was the most fun thing he did with his siblings, and it taught him the value of teamwork and critical thinking with all the puzzle-solving involved. He wanted to teach the same to his kids and decided to carry forward this tradition. He added his own twist to the whole gig. To instill a healthy reading habit in his kids, he would give them a book to read and base the treasure hunt's clues on the story. If they read the book, they would easily be able to solve the clues; if not, they may never reach their intended treasure! His kids loved the challenge and he loved seeing them put their heads together to solve it.

THE POWER OF FAMILY TRADITIONS

You would be surprised to know how powerful family traditions are in creating lasting memories and teaching valuable lessons. Fun activities, such as those described above, can be such powerful ways of teaching your children values like hard work, resilience, critical thinking, and team spirit.

Family traditions also provide the much-needed anchor to your children, which they can rely on in times of difficulty or when they need to power through while dealing with emotionally overwhelming situations.

You can build your own traditions or carry forward the ones you grew up with. Every family is different but the best part about it is that you get to be creative. Building trust and a strong bond between yourself and your children will bring you the ultimate satisfaction of raising another human being. Traditions are also great when it comes to creating shared experiences. A family that experiences life together grows together!

Let's have a look at some of the ways in which you can do this:

- **You can work to incorporate your cultural and family traditions from your childhood into your family's present life.** For example, if you remember something special your family did around the holidays, you can find ways to carry on with that.
- **Be creative and authentic when connecting with your roots.** Allow enough space for your kids to also come up with creative ideas on how they would like to spend traditional holidays and incorporate their suggestions into your plans.
- **Plan out holidays, special seasonal hikes, or trips for your family.** Anything that changes your surroundings becomes an excellent opportunity to have different experiences and see how you fare as a family unit!
- **If it works for you, you can plan educational trips, and I don't mean just the museum!** For example, places that are famous for manufacturing or producing something specific, whether food-related or crafts like ceramics, can be great places to learn about the diversity of life.
- **You can also get your children (yourself and your partner included!) into the habit of reflecting on their experiences after special events, trips, or holidays!** Journaling is a great way to see what each kid's main takeaway is from the shared experience and give insights into what your children love. This can further give you ideas about your next plans. What's not to love?

The list really is endless, but you get the point. Carrying forward your own traditions and making new ones is what enriches our lives beyond mere survival. It makes our lives sweeter. If you and your partner are the orchestrating figures behind the fun and stimulating activities for your kids, you're both bound to become the world's best parents.

BRINGING SOMETHING SPECIAL TO DAILY SCHEDULES

The fun activities don't have to be limited to holiday times only. The best habits are formed with daily repetitions and by following a fruitful routine. I understand that planning something extraordinary takes a lot of time and energy, which, let's be honest, is not always possible with the kind of responsibilities parents deal with.

However, that is exactly the thing! Daily traditions or routines don't have to be something big or extraordinary for them to be special. For example, a simple thing like making a rule of having one meal of the day together isn't that difficult. For something to be special and meaningful, you only need to believe and treat it as something special, and it will become so.

An important thing to remember here is that these schedules are not just for your kids to cultivate good habits but also to give them a sense of certainty in terms of what to expect each day. That predictability allows them to settle down and function from a place of feeling secure. It also helps them trust that you will be there for them and they can come to you if they have anything to share or need your guidance on.

Again, there is a lot of space for you to creatively devise what works best for your family; here are some examples that can point you in that direction:

- crafting simple daily rituals that build stronger connections with your kids
- being present for bedtime and reading stories to them
- having a heart-to-heart about their day
- helping them do their homework
- special weekend fun including movies or short-trips
- supporting them in whatever hobbies they choose for themselves and encouraging them to explore more
- Show appreciation when they create something for you, like sketches or drawings (children are fond of scribbling away to glory!)
- getting fun and dirty with them when they ask you to play with them or taking the initiative yourself

Giving your time and attention to your kids is the best way to ensure they feel connected to you. If you're not afraid to play in the mud with them, they are sure to think of you as the best dad in the whole wide world!

PASSING DOWN VALUES

Alas, parenting is about passing down core values and wisdom to your child so they may live meaningful lives and be responsible members of society. Parents are the first teacher's children encounter. From the earliest interactions with your baby to the deep conversations you will have when your baby grows into a young adult, your teachings will play a fundamental part in deciding your child's moral compass.

At this point, it is equally important to highlight that children are keen observers and absorb verbal, as well as non-verbal, cues from their environment. So, as much as you would be consciously teaching your child valuable lessons, much of their behavior will also be shaped by your own behavior and example. As they say, teaching by example is the best kind of teaching.

Therefore, the way you act when you are upset, the way you process disagreements and anger, the way you show resilience, the way you appreciate and show gratitude to your family, your child will absorb everything. There are a few directions you can take here to ensure you are imparting the best to your child.

Firstly, one of the best-known ways to pass down important lessons is through storytelling and engaging in critical thinking. When you narrate something to your child, make sure to ask about their opinions on why something that happened was right or wrong or how some character's actions were good or bad. Then, make it a point to gently explain to them why something is right or wrong.

Remember, we saw in the previous chapter how the most effective parenting styles involve not only setting rules and enforcing them but also explaining to your child why these rules are important in the first place. Similarly, with anything that you teach your child, whether directly or through storytelling, there is a higher likelihood of them understanding the difference between right and wrong if they understand the reason behind it.

Secondly, lead by example. The values of kindness, forgiveness, patience, and honesty are best taught through your own practice of them. Let me paint you a picture. Imagine you are running late for work and have an important presentation coming up. You decide to take a final look at some important facts as you quickly rush through breakfast. You have kept your documents on the table and your kid is around at the same time, having his breakfast before school. Because kids are kids, his morning energy causes him to run around and spill some juice on the table, ruining your papers. You don't have the time to get another set of printouts. You're furious. What do you do?

You can either yell at your kid for not being careful at the breakfast table. Or, you can show restraint and patience in that moment, even when it's difficult. As a parent, you have the responsibility to realize that your child will likely do things that require consequences that he does not yet understand. It is on you to gently make him realize why this was potentially harmful. When you sit down with your child calmly, and explain the reason why this could cause trouble for you at work and how it will make you sad, your child can understand why he is being asked to be careful. Such lessons go a long way in constructively teaching them by example.

Thirdly, be present. Show up in places where you are expected, whether they are the parent-teacher meetings, important games, their school drama performances, or sporting events. In fact, be engaged with your child and help them practice for it. If it's a fancy dress competition, help your child look the best character! If it's a soccer game, help them prepare for it. You get the idea!

Fourthly, share your own life experiences with your child as he grows up. Tell them of the times you felt directionless or depressed, as well as what helped you build your resilience. Of course, the point is not to compare or give instructions in a condescending tone. The point is to reassure them that they've got this and everyone goes through tough times. Show them you care and you will always have their back no matter what. This will create a safe and accepting environment in your home, which can help your child open up about their own life—especially as they enter early adulthood. *Always make space for them to voice their dreams and goals and help them like you're their partner in wanting to achieve what is best for them.*

Fifthly, teach them to be self-reliant in things, to build and fix things on their own as much as possible. It is an important life skill that will serve them well when they go out into the world to live on their own.

Lastly, don't forget to teach them a sense of gratitude and a practice of positive self-talk with affirmations. As much as we want our kids to be protected from the harshness of the world, they will inevitably encounter them. Instead of keeping our kids caged in and sheltered, your job as a father is to prepare them to face all of life's challenges with resilience.

With that, here you are. Now, go out there and be the best dad in the world to your baby and the best partner to your wife. You've got this, Dad!

CONCLUSION

We began our journey by acknowledging the transformational experience of having a baby grace your life. And now, we end it with the knowledge of how that transformation occurs.

We have seen the physical, mental, and emotional changes your partner undergoes through the nine months of pregnancy to figure out how your baby grows before entering the world. We have also seen how a baby will bring changes to your life and schedule, requiring you to balance your work and family life.

Remaining open to and curious about the pregnancy journey will allow you to appreciate the different phases and opportunities you will get to deepen your relationship with your partner. With open and honest communication, as well as lots of patience and care, you can create the perfect support system for your partner as you both face the nine months together as a team.

Additionally, the more you educate yourself on your shared philosophy of birth, make a birth plan with your partner, and make informed decisions about how you want your baby's birth to be handled, the more you will feel completely involved in the process.

With the ideas discussed here, you can confidently navigate the roles and responsibilities of fatherhood. You have all the tools you need to prepare your home for your little one, survive the newborn phase with diaper and feeding duty, assist your partner in childcare responsibilities, and effectively co-parent with the best possible parenting approach for your baby.

Importantly, we have also seen the crucial role rest and self-care play in being a good father. A baby will require your constant attention and care, and sometimes juggling that with work can become supremely overwhelming. But, if you're burnt out, you cannot be meaningfully present for your baby and family. Therefore, taking time to rejuvenate yourself is just as important as being present for your family. Striking that balance is key to achieving a healthy work-life balance.

Finally, we have also seen how parenting is about forging emotional bonds and imparting core values and wisdom to your child so that they know everything that you know, which will help them move through the world and live a fulfilling life.

For all the times you have doubted yourself, know that parenting is not a skill you learn once and that's it. It is an ever-evolving job and has a learning curve to it. There is no one way of doing it right. Your best guide is your love for your baby and your desire to give them the best. Yes, it will require you to learn and grow as a parent too, but that is true for everything we do in life. You can do it! Go be an awesome dad!

FIRST TIME DAD SURVIVAL GUIDE

Now you have everything you need to be the world's best father, it's time to pass on your new found knowledge and show other readers where they can find the same help.

Simply by leaving your honest opinion of this book on Amazon, you'll show other first time dad's where they can find the information they're looking for, and pass their passion for becoming a supportive spouse and great father.

Thank you for your help. Supporting other First Time Fathers is kept alive when we pass on our knowledge – and you're helping us to do just that.

REFERENCES

A quote by John Wilmot. (n.d.). Goodreads. https://www.goodreads.com/quotes/tag/fatherhood

Abedin, S. (2022, September 11). *The basics of water birth.* WebMD. https://www.webmd.com/baby/water-birth

Abraham, E., Hendler, T., Shapira-Lichter, I., Kanat-Maymon, Y., Zagoory-Sharon, O., & Feldman, R. (2014). Father's brain is sensitive to childcare experiences. *Proceedings of the National Academy of Sciences, 111*(27), 9792–9797. https://doi.org/10.1073/pnas.1402569111

Bakermans-Kranenburg, M. J., Lotz, A., Alyousefi-van Dijk, K., & IJzendoorn, M. (2019, October 14). Birth of a father: Fathering in the first 1,000 days. *Child Development Perspectives, 13*(4), 247–253. https://doi.org/10.1111/cdep.12347

Behson, S., & Robbins, N. (2016, May). *The effects of involved fatherhood on families, and how fathers can be supported both at the workplace and in the home.* United Nations. https://www.un.org/esa/socdev/family/docs/egm16/BehsonRobbins.pdf

Brown, S. (2022, August 27). *How to change a diaper: Step-by-step instructions.* Verywell Family. https://www.verywellfamily.com/how-to-change-a-diaper-289239

Calmus, T. (2022). *A dude's guide to baby size.* WaterBrook

Campoamor, D. (2016, October 19). *7 dads describe what it felt like to hold their baby for the first time.* Romper. https://www.romper.com/p/7-dads-describe-what-it-felt-like-to-hold-their-baby-for-the-first-time-20475

Christiano, D. (2023, February 7). *Baby feeding schedule: A guide to the first year.* Healthline. https://www.healthline.com/health/parenting/baby-feeding-schedule

Cleveland Clinic. (2018, January 1). *Pregnancy: Physical changes after delivery.* Cleveland Clinic. https://my.clevelandclinic.org/health/articles/9682-pregnancy-physical-changes-after-delivery

Cleveland Clinic. (2021, October 7). *Breech baby.* Cleveland Clinic. https://my.clevelandclinic.org/health/diseases/21848-breech-baby

Cleveland Clinic. (2022, May 10). *Braxton hicks contractions*. Cleveland Clinic. https://my.clevelandclinic.org/health/symptoms/22965-braxton-hicks

Cleveland Clinic. (2023, June 9). *Colic*. Cleveland Clinic. https://my.cleveland clinic.org/health/diseases/10823-colic

Crider, C. (2021, April 30). *What to expect at 9 months pregnant*. Healthline. https://www.healthline.com/health/pregnancy/9-months-pregnant

Domenica. (2016, July 19). *16 creative ways to record your pregnancy*. Mum's Grapevine. https://mumsgrapevine.com.au/2016/07/pregnancy-memories/

Donaldson-Evans, C. (2023a, October 5). *1 and 2 weeks pregnant*. What to Expect. https://www.whattoexpect.com/pregnancy/week-by-week/weeks-1-and-2.aspx

Donaldson-Evans, C. (2023b, October 5). *13 weeks pregnant*. What to Expect. https://www.whattoexpect.com/pregnancy/week-by-week/week-13.aspx

Donaldson-Evans, C. (2023c, October 5). *20 weeks pregnant*. What to Expect. https://www.whattoexpect.com/pregnancy/week-by-week/week-20.aspx

Donaldson-Evans, C. (2023d, October 5). *24 weeks pregnant*. What to Expect. https://www.whattoexpect.com/pregnancy/week-by-week/week-24.aspx

Downs, M. (2014, September 17). *New dads: What to expect after baby arrives*. WebMD. https://www.webmd.com/parenting/baby/features/new-dads-what-to-expect

FamilyEducation. (n.d.). *What's expected of new dads?* Family Education. https://www.familyeducation.com/babies/growth-development/whats-expected-new-dads

Geddes, J. K. (2021, January 6). *How to soothe a crying baby*. What to Expect. https://www.whattoexpect.com/first-year/care/how-to-make-baby-stop-crying

Geddes, J. K. (2022, August 12). *How to babyproof every room of the house*. What to Expect. https://www.whattoexpect.com/nursery-decorating/child proofing-basics.aspx

Gettler, L. T., Kuo, P. X., Sarma, M. S., Trumble, B. C., Burke Lefever, J. E., & Braungart-Rieker, J. M. (2021, April 16). Fathers' oxytocin responses to first holding their newborns: Interactions with testosterone reactivity to predict later parenting behavior and father-infant bonds. *Developmental Psychobiology, 63*(5), 1384–1398. https://doi.org/10.1002/dev.22121

Glassdoor. (2022, May 4). *Creating a better work-life balance as a new dad*. Glassdoor. https://www.glassdoor.com/blog/creating-better-work-life-balance-as-a-new-dad/

Gurevich, R. (2021, October 26). *What is the Bradley method?* Verywell Family. https://www.verywellfamily.com/the-bradley-method-4586903

Hirsch, A. S. (2023, May 4). *From work/life balance to work/life integration.* SHRM. https://www.shrm.org/resourcesandtools/hr-topics/employee-relations/pages/from-worklife-balance-to-worklife-integration.aspx

Holland, K. (2019, March 22). *Sex after birth: What to expect and how long to wait.* Healthline. https://www.healthline.com/health/pregnancy/sex-after-birth

Iftikhar, N. (2020, June 27). *How to Know When to Go to the Hospital for Labor.* Healthline. https://www.healthline.com/health/pregnancy/when-to-go-to-the-hospital-for-labor

Jezard, A. (2018, January 3). *Millennial fathers are rejecting the "bad dad" stereotypes.* World Economic Forum. https://www.weforum.org/agenda/2018/01/millennial-fathers-are-rejecting-on-screen-dad-stereotypes-research-finds/

John Hopkins Medicine. (n.d.). *Nutrition during pregnancy.* https://www.hopkinsmedicine.org/health/wellness-and-prevention/nutrition-during-pregnancy

Karp, H. (n.d.). *The 5 S's for Soothing Babies.* Happiest Baby. https://www.happiestbaby.com/blogs/baby/the-5-s-s-for-soothing-babies

Katz, R. (2022, July 28). *3 ways to exercise your parent rights to advocate for your kid.* PBS SoCal. https://www.pbssocal.org/education/parent-education-rights-3-ways-you-can-advocate-for-your-kid

Lamaze International. (n.d.). *Our history.* https://www.lamaze.org/about-lamaze

Lansford, J. E. (2021, June 15). *The importance of fathers for child development.* Psychology Today. https://www.psychologytoday.com/intl/blog/parenting-and-culture/202106/the-importance-fathers-child-development

Lascurain, K. (2020, August 8). *How to baby-proof your nursery.* Verywell Family. https://www.verywellfamily.com/how-to-baby-proof-your-nursery-2504923

Leech, J. (2023, April 25). *10 top benefits of getting more sleep.* Healthline. https://www.healthline.com/nutrition/10-reasons-why-good-sleep-is-important#6.-Poor-sleep-is-linked-to-depression

Lewsley, J. (2021, March). *11 ways to survive stress in pregnancy.* BabyCentre

UK. https://www.babycentre.co.uk/a552044/11-ways-to-survive-stress-in-pregnancy

Lyubykh, Z., & Gulseren, D. B. (2023, May 31). *How to take better breaks at work, according to research.* Harvard Business Review. https://hbr.org/2023/05/how-to-take-better-breaks-at-work-according-to-research

Mayer, B. A. (2020, August 21). *How the internet affects your mental wellbeing.* Healthline. https://www.healthline.com/health/the-mental-health-effects-of-being-constantly-online#A-surge-in-screens

Mayo Clinic. (2022a, January 13). *Stages of Labor and birth: Baby, it's time!* https://www.mayoclinic.org/healthy-lifestyle/labor-and-delivery/in-depth/stages-of-labor/art-20046545

Mayo Clinic. (2022b, March 8). *1st trimester pregnancy: What to expect.* https://www.mayoclinic.org/healthy-lifestyle/pregnancy-week-by-week/in-depth/pregnancy/art-20047208

Mayo Clinic. (2022c, March 9). *Second trimester pregnancy: What to expect.* https://www.mayoclinic.org/healthy-lifestyle/pregnancy-week-by-week/in-depth/pregnancy/art-20047732

Miller, C. C. (2023, March 13). Fathers gained family time in the pandemic. many don't want to give it back. *The New York Times.* https://www.nytimes.com/2023/03/12/upshot/fathers-pandemic-remote-work.html

Morin, A. (2022, August 9). *4 types of parenting styles and their effects on kids.* Verywell Family. https://www.verywellfamily.com/types-of-parenting-styles-1095045

Nielsen, L. (2023). *Myths and lies about dads: How they hurt us all.* Routledge.

OASH. (2021, February 22). *Stages of pregnancy.* Office on Women's Health. https://www.womenshealth.gov/pregnancy/youre-pregnant-now-what/stages-pregnancy

Parenting NI. (2018, October 25). *Parent-Child relationship - why it's important.* Parenting NI. https://www.parentingni.org/blog/parent-child-relationship-why-its-important/

Parker, W. (2022, October 5). *How to help your partner through the last month of pregnancy.* Verywell Family. https://www.verywellfamily.com/making-it-through-last-pregnancy-month-1270769

Patrick. (n.d.). *20+ essential self-care tips and activities for dads.* Daddy Simply. https://daddysimply.com/self-care-ideas-for-dads-recharge-and-refresh/

Rudick, J. A., & Brott, A. A. (2021). *The expectant father: The ultimate guide for dads-to-be* (5th ed.). WW Norton.

Schnabolk, L. C. (2023, October 30). *What happens right after baby is born?* The Bump. https://www.thebump.com/a/what-happens-after-the-baby-is-born

Stanford Medicine Children's Health. (n.d.). *Newborn sleep patterns.* https://www.stanfordchildrens.org/en/topic/default?id=newborn-sleep-patterns-90-P02632

Starrick, S. (2023, April 4). *How to advocate for your child: Lessons from a powerful parent.* Jai Institute for Parenting. https://www.jaiinstituteforparenting.com/how-to-advocate-for-your-child-lessons-from-a-powerful-parent

Stewart, R. (2016, June 14). *Soon-to-be dads: How to help – and what not to say – during pregnancy.* UTSouthwestern Medical Center. https://utswmed.org/medblog/fathers-guide-to-pregnancy/

Stickler, T. (2020, July 9). *Maintaining a healthy pregnancy.* Healthline. https://www.healthline.com/health/pregnancy/healthy-pregnancy#prenatal-care

Suni, E. (2023, October 20). *Sleep training.* Sleep Foundation. https://www.sleepfoundation.org/baby-sleep/sleep-training

Sutherland, A. (2014, April 9). *How parental conflict hurts kids.* Institute for Family Studies. https://ifstudies.org/blog/how-parental-conflict-hurts-kids

Swanson, W. S. (2023, August 24). *The baby poop guide: What's normal and what's not.* Parents. https://www.parents.com/baby/diapers/dirty/the-scoop-on-poop-whats-normal-whats-not/

Taylor, M. (2023, July 25). *How to swaddle your baby.* What to Expect. https://www.whattoexpect.com/first-year/baby-care/baby-care-101/secrets-to-swaddling.aspx

UNICEF. (2023, January 27). *Skin-to-skin contact.* UNICEF UK. https://www.unicef.org.uk/babyfriendly/baby-friendly-resources/implementing-standards-resources/skin-to-skin-contact/

WebMD. (2023, July 12). *What to know about parental burnout.* WebMD. https://www.webmd.com/parenting/what-to-know-about-parental-burnout

Wooll, M. (2022, December 28). *Work-Life Integration: What It Is And 5 Ways to Develop It.* BetterUp. https://www.betterup.com/blog/work-life-integration

Zimlich, R. (2021, May 21). *What you need to know about giving birth.* Verywell Health. https://www.verywellhealth.com/giving-birth-5179932